Next: Young American Writers on the New Generation (editor)

THE ACCIDENTAL ASIAN

THE
ACCIDENTAL
ASIAN

Notes

of a

Native

Speaker

ERIC LIU

Random House
New York

Library of Congress Cataloging-in-Publication Data
Liu, Eric.
The accidental Asian : notes of a native speaker / Eric Liu. — 1st ed.
p.   cm.
ISBN 0-679-44862-4
1. Liu, Eric.   2. Chinese Americans—Biography.   3. Asian
Americans—Race identity.   4. Asian Americans—Cultural
assimilation.   5. Asian Americans—Politics and government.
6. United States—Race relations.   I. Title.
E184.C5L62   1998
305.8951'073—dc21   97-44243

Random House website address: www.randomhouse.com
Printed in the United States of America on acid-free paper
2 4 6 8 9 7 5 3
First Edition

Book design by Oksana Kushnir

For my family

Contents

THE ACCIDENTAL ASIAN

Song
for
My Father

1.

By my bed, gathering a little dust now, I'm afraid, is a small
paperback book. I've kept it there ever since it was published four or five years ago, and it's become one of those
things in my apartment that I see every day without seeing anymore. On top of the paperback book is a thin pamphlet, *The
Healing of Mind and Soul in the Twenty-third Psalm,* given to
me by a friend of the family, Pastor Wan. Beneath the paperback is a study Bible, New International Version, also given to
me by the pastor, and a Dover edition of the Book of Psalms.

I'm not a religious person; or, rather, I wasn't raised to be a
religious person: never belonged to a church, never became
acquainted with the grammar and word of the Good Book. But
over the years, there have been more than a few occasions

---

when I've read that pamphlet, that Bible, and those psalms in earnest, finding in their allegories and metaphors something short of grace, perhaps, but something greater than mere solace.

So it's no accident that in this stack of salves I've included this slender paperback. It is unlike any other book I own. On the cover, set against a faded backdrop of his own handwriting, is a color photograph of my father. In the photograph, taken sometime in the 1960s, my father's head is turned to his left, his mouth slightly open in a relaxed smile. Even behind heavy-framed glasses, his eyes appear to be seeing something clearly. It seems he might be saying something soon, something thoughtful, or maybe playful. A lock of his black hair, bunched like wet grass, has fallen out of place, sweeping across his fore-head. His skin, still smooth and full, tells me he was a young man not that many years before the picture was taken. But his visage—knowing, kind, self-aware—tells me he has already become the man I knew as Baba. That picture is why I keep the paperback at my bedside. It keeps my father close, sets his gaze upon me as I sleep.

The book was compiled by several of my father's child-hood friends after he died in 1991. This wasn't, as far as I know, some sort of Chinese tradition, publishing a memorial book for a departed chum. It was just an act of loyalty; of love, if I may say that. In part, the book is a record of grief, containing the obituary from the *Poughkeepsie Journal*, my eulogy, an elegiac essay by my mother. But for most of its 198 pages, it is actually a prose reunion, a memoir of the idyllic adolescence of a band of boys in postwar Taiwan.

There are pieces in the book, written by my father and his brothers and his classmates, about high school life, about a favorite teacher, about camping and fishing trips, about picaresque adventures where nary an adult appears. There are photographs too; in many of them, Dad and his friends are wearing their school uniforms, baggy and vaguely military. One snapshot I remember vividly. Eight or nine of them are walking up a dirt road, jesting and smiling. And there's my father at the end of this happy phalanx—khaki hat a bit too big, arm pumping jauntily and foot raised in mid-march, singing a song. The face is my father's, but the stance, so utterly carefree, is hardly recognizable. I stared at that picture for a long time when I first got the book.

It's through these photographs that I'll read the book every so often, searching the scenes for new revelations. That's partly because the photographs are so wonderful, soft black-and-white images of an innocence beyond articulation. But it's also, frankly, because I do not understand the text. Almost all the entries, you see, are written in Chinese—a language that I once could read and write with middling proficiency but have since let slip into disuse. Though I know enough to read from top to bottom, right to left, and "back" to "front," I recognize so few of the characters now that perusing the text yields little more than frustration, and shame. I know what the book contains only because Mom has told me. And she's had to tell me several times.

On one or two occasions I've sat down with my pocket Chinese-English dictionary, determined to decipher at least the essays that my father wrote. This was painstaking work and I never got very far. For each Chinese character, I first had to determine the ideographic root, then count the brush strokes, then turn to an index ordered by root and by number of strokes, then match the character, then figure out its romanized spelling, then look up its definition. By the time I solved one word, I'd already forgotten the previous one. Meaning was hard enough to determine; context was even more elusive.

So it is, I sometimes think, with my father's life. On the one hand, it's easy to locate my father and my family in the grand narrative of "the Chinese American experience." On the other hand, it doesn't take long for this narrative to seem more like a riddle than a fable. Leafing through the pages of the memorial book, staring dumbly at their blur of ideographs, I realize just how little I know about those years of Baba's life before he arrived in America, and before I arrived in the world. I sense how difficult it is to be literate in another man's life, how opaque an inheritance one's identity truly is. I begin to perceive my own ignorance of self.

When Chao-hua Liu came to the United States in 1955, at the age of eighteen, he was Chinese. When he died thirty-six

years later, he was, I'd say, something other than Chinese. And
he had helped raise a son who was Chinese in perhaps only a
nominal sense. But what, ultimately, does all this mean?
Where does this Chineseness reside? In the word? In the deed?
In what is learned—or what is already known? And how is it
passed from one generation to the next? Some of the answers
lie, I know, in a book I am still unable to read. But there are
other answers, I suspect, in a book I must now begin to write.

2.

If I could render as a painting the image I have of my father as
a young man, it would be a post-impressionist work, late
Cézanne, rather than a work of realist precision. Actually, it
would be more like an *unfinished* Cézanne: blocks of color;
indistinct shapes; and then, suddenly, great swaths of blank
canvas. The scraps of knowledge I have of my father's pre-
American life come from letters he wrote, from my mother's
secondhand memories, from family lore. They aren't random
fragments, exactly. But they aren't full-fledged stories either.
They're more like scenes, symbolic images that can be
arranged in rough sequence yet still resist narration.

Here is some of what I know about my Chinese father:
That he was the second of six brothers, born in Nanjing in
1936. That his father was a pilot and a general whose given

name, Guo Yun, translates roughly as Deliverance of the Nation. That he fled in the night with his family to Taiwan when Communist forces had advanced too close. That when he was a boy, he raised pigeons in a cage on the roof of his house and then one day set them all free. That he was ill for a lengthy period as a child, but took the opportunity of being bedridden to read the Chinese classics over and over again. That the medication he took would prove, years later, to have damaged his kidneys. That his father's driver taught him how to drive a jeep at age twelve, or maybe thirteen. That his family's cook taught him how to make dumplings. That he was an outstanding student and mischievous, though mischievous in the safe, authority-affirming way of an outstanding student. That he left his home and his country after high school.

It is typical, I suppose, that the second generation forgets to ask the first generation why it became the first. But is it typical, as well, to accept without comment what few recollections the first generation offers? Or was it simply my own lack of curiosity? I never knew, for instance, that Baba was born in Nanjing until I was applying to college and needed to fill in the space for "Father's Birthplace." I never knew whether he, the son of a general, felt pressure to join the military. I never knew why he set those pigeons free. I never knew how Confucius and Mencius had influenced him, although he told my mother that they had. I never knew whether he was bitter about the bad medicine. I never knew where he drove once he learned to drive. I never knew what ambitions he packed with him when he sailed across the Pacific. I never knew whether he was homesick when he cooked his first meal in America.

My knowledge of Baba's years in China and Taiwan is like a collection of souvenirs, but of souvenirs that don't belong to me. They evoke a milieu; they signify something. But sifting through them, I cannot be sure whether the story they tell is simply the story I've chosen to imagine. If I were a fiction writer, I could manipulate these scenes a hundred different ways. I could tell you a tale and pass it off as emblematic of Baba's childhood, of wartime China, of the Chinese condition. Even as an essayist, I impute significance to the scenes in a way that reveals as much about my own yearnings as it does about my father's. It is the Heisenberg principle of remembrance: the mere act of observing a memory changes that memory's meaning.

This truth, that we unwittingly mold other people's pasts to our own ends, is easy to grasp on an individual level—especially when the individual is a son searching sentimentally for his father. On a collective level, though, it becomes rather less obvious. Nation, race, diaspora—all these are communities of collective memory, and the greater the community, the more occluded are its motives for remembering. For people who think of themselves as "a people," the hard facts of history tend to melt into folklore, which dissolves into aesthetic, which evaporates like mist into race-consciousness. What matters, after a while, is not the memory of shared experience so much as the shared experience of memory.

Consider the mythology of the Overseas Chinese, which is how people in China and Taiwan refer to the thirty million or so ethnic Chinese who live elsewhere. The idea is simple: there is China, which is filled with Chinese; and there is the rest of the world, which, to varying degrees, is sprinkled with Chinese. The ethnocentrism is manifest, the essentialism unapologetic: "You can take a Chinese out of China, but you can't take the China out of a Chinese."

But just what is it that binds together these millions of Chinese outside China? Well, it's their Chineseness. And what is Chineseness? That which binds together the Chinese. Entire conferences and scholarly tomes have been devoted to this catechism, with roughly the same results. Granted, there exists, in the form of a rich culture and history, what political scientist Samuel Huntington would call a "core Sinic civilization." That civilization, however, isn't *intrinsic* to people of Chinese genotype; it is transmitted—or not. And whether it is transmitted to the Overseas Chinese depends, ultimately, on consent rather than descent. Chineseness isn't a mystical, more authentic way of being; it's just a decision to act Chinese.

Which, of course, only raises more questions. Though my father, in the first eighteen years of his life, was Chinese and nothing but Chinese; though his were the actions of a Chinese person, it is difficult to isolate which aspects of his values and behavior you would specifically call "Chinese." True, he believed in the importance of family and the value of education. He was respectful toward his elders. He was self-disciplined and intellectually rigorous. He was even-tempered, not a rebellious spirit. He appreciated the beauty of Chinese painting and the wisdom of Chinese poetry. He loved reading and writing Chinese. He enjoyed eating Chinese food.

This is beginning to sound, though, like a piece of inductive reasoning: working in reverse from a general notion of what it means to "act Chinese" in order to identify a particular personality *as Chinese*. One problem with such backward reasoning is that it views colorless attributes through a tinted lens, turning a trait like even-temperedness into a sure sign of Chineseness. Another is that it filters out evidence that contradicts the conclusion: there was plenty about Dad, after all, that didn't fit anybody's stereotype of "Chinese character." That may be hard to tell when my indistinct image of him is set against a faded Chinese backdrop. It becomes more apparent in the context I knew him in: the context of America.

3.

Another photograph, this one dated April 1962. It's a black-and-white shot, slightly out of focus, set in a spare apartment. There is no art on the walls, not even a calendar. The curtains are thin, a diaphanous membrane that can't quite contain the light outside. In the center of the picture is my father, sitting at a desk with stacks of papers and books. He is leaning back slightly in a stiff wooden chair, his left leg crossed, and he is reading a book that rests easily on his knee. He is wearing a sweatshirt emblazoned with ILLINOIS and a Stars and Stripes shield. He is smoking a pipe, which he holds to his mouth absently with his right hand.

When I first saw this picture, it put me in mind of a daguerreotype image I'd once seen of an 1890s Yale student sitting in his room. The settings, of course, couldn't have been more different. That Yale room, with its dark wood paneling and clubby leather chairs, walls adorned with undergraduate paraphernalia, was the domain of a Gilded Age heir. My father's room was the kind of place one rightly calls a *flat*. Yet for all the obvious differences in scene, there was, in both my father and that long-ago Yalie, the same self-conscious manner. *We are Serious Young Men*, their contemplative poses announce, *and we are preparing for the Future.*

Maybe it's just the pipe and the college sweatshirt, or the posture. Still, I can't help thinking that my father in this photograph looks—what? Not quite so Chinese, I suppose. When this shot was taken, he'd already been in the United States for over seven years. He'd worked odd jobs to save money. One of them, my personal favorite, was painting the yellow line down the middle of a South Dakota highway. He had become, during this period, a devotee of Hank Williams and Muhammad Ali. He'd earned a degree in philosophy—Western philosophy—from the University of Illinois, and had become fascinated with Camus and existentialism. He had finished a master's in mathematics. He had been dating my mother, whom he'd met at a picnic with other students from Taiwan, for three years. They would be married a year later.

Their wedding, from what my mother has told me, was a fairly accurate measure of where they were in life then: not quite in the mainstream, but so happy to have each other's company, so much in a world of their own, that little else mattered. The ceremony took place in a church, because that was where weddings took place in America. Except for the officiant and a few others, almost everyone there was Chinese. Still, there were no traditional Chinese rituals; no ancestor worship or kowtowing or burning of incense. They spoke their vows in English. The bride wore white, the groom a rented black tuxedo. The reception was in the church basement. The honeymoon, in rural Michigan. It was the end of November.

I wonder how people regarded them, these young newlyweds. To your average citizen of rural Michigan, this slight, black-haired couple probably looked like exchange students or tourists: like foreigners. To me, they look heartbreakingly American. Indeed, this hopeful phase—this period of composing a life to the rhythms of a new country—is far easier for me to conjure up than their years in China and Taiwan. There are more photographs, for one thing, more anecdotes to help sharpen my impressions. There are familiar names and places too, like Ann Arbor, Millbrook, Bennett College. But more than all that, there is the familiar idiom of progress—the steady sense of climbing, and climbing higher; of forgetting, and forgetting more.

In our archetype of the immigrant experience, it is the first generation that remains wedded to the ways of the Old Country and the second generation that forsakes them. This, we learn, is the tragedy of assimilation: the inevitable estrangement between the immigrant father who imagines himself still in exile and the American son who strains to prove his belonging. There is, I'll admit, a certain dramatic appeal to this account. There is also, unfortunately, a good deal of contrivance. In search of narrative tension, we let ourselves forget that the father, too, is transformed. We let ourselves think of the first generation's life as a mere chrysalis, an interlude between the larval existence of the homeland and the fully formed Americanness of the second generation. But the truth is that the father can sometimes become his own form of butterfly.

In Baba's case, the metamorphosis found its most vivid expression in language. Even as a teenager in Taiwan he had excelled in his English classes. Once he came to the States he picked up jargon, slang, and idiom with a collector's enthusiasm. IBM, which he joined after grad school and where he worked for twenty-seven years, was both a great source and a constant testing ground for his American vernacular. It gave him, for instance, his favorite acronym—SNAFU—which, he loved to remind us, stood for Situation Normal: All Fucked Up.

I think Baba's facility with English is part of what gave me such a powerful sense when I was growing up that he wasn't quite like other Chinese immigrants. Other Chinese immigrants, it seemed, spoke English as if it was Chinese, using *he* and *she* interchangeably, ignoring the conjugation of verbs, not bothering to make nouns plural. My father's English was several tiers better than that; more important, he spoke the language with relish, as if he owned it.

He did have an accent, although for the life of me now, I can't describe it or reproduce it. In fact, I remember being surprised once when a friend said something about the Chinese inflection of my father's English: the same sense of surprise I'd had as a boy when I saw myself and my friends in a mirror and realized how much shorter I was than they were. I simply didn't hear his accent.

What I heard was the way he was fluent in American small talk, the way he got a kick out of backhanded compliments and cornball humor. What I heard was the way he would fixate delightedly on phrases that he'd pick up here and there. "What a joke" was a refrain he learned from my friend George. "I mean business!" he got from an auto-repair ad on television. "I yield to the congresswoman from Old English Way" was how, after watching the parliamentary theater of the Iran-contra hearings, he would pass the phone to Mom when I called home. What I heard too was how well he could argue in English, angrily, when a repairman tried to rip him off.

His command of written English was also surprisingly good. When I was in high school Baba would edit my writing assignments for clarity and logic. When my sister Andrea was in high school, and was editor of the newspaper, he would actually write short unsigned columns just to help her fill up ink space. He would opine for 300 words about the death penalty or student apathy or some such pressing topic with sincerity and just a touch of goofiness.

That same combination marked the handful of letters that Baba ever wrote to me. The letters are markedly different from the formal and correct business memos he would produce for work; they are relaxed, sprinkled with grammatical slips, as if he were just talking to me at home. One of these letters he wrote during my first months after college, when I had moved to Washington, and it may be the clearest recording of his voice that I have. I imagine him at the kitchen table, pipe in hand perhaps, writing to me:

10/28/90

Dear Eric,

Enclosed are your recent mails. You probably should change mailing address for Yale Alumni Magazine and Columbia House CD Club. Otherwise, you may run the risk of receiving history by the time we get around to forwarding it to you. (We are so behind in handling our mails)

16

Today is the day the clock "Falls Back" by one hour. It's one O'Clock A.M. But actually it's only 12:00. Both Mom and I are so fortunate to have this extra hour to do our mails. The rest of the evening was all used up in reading the Chinese newspaper.—the most time consuming thing in the Liu's family! We may have to, for the second time, stop our subscription of the World Journal so we can have a little breathing room to straighten out our daily life around the house. What do you say?

Suddenly it turned into winter in the last two days. Yesterday I worked in the City. I walked from Grand Central to 590 Madison Ave (20 min walk). It was cold. We had freeze warning. What a joke. Half of the leaves are still on the trees in green color in our back yard. They could be frozen there for the rest of their lifes. And that's not a bad idea. Imagine I don't have to sweep the leaves!

Everything is OK at home. Mom & I are eating more hot Chinese food, since we now don't have to worry about one member of the Liu's family who cannot handle the hot stuff at the dinner table. Mom feels strongly that I should dress more impressively as I start my new assignment in the City. Today we went to Galaria to buy a new pair of black shoes (Like yours) and a new briefcase. It looks classy. I mean business!

Our hiking trip got delayed two weekends in a roll. Now it feels like winter. It's probably good-bye hiking trip this year. Last Sunday was a real nice day. Mom and I had our own hiking trip walking from Old English Way to the Village & back.

Is everything OK with you? Be careful with the cold weather that's approaching fast. Dress warm in the morning when you go out to the subway station. Alternatively, put on some body fat.

All for now. Take care. Mom say Hi.

Love, Dad

4.

My mother says that Baba's Chinese, actually, was first-rate, as good as that of any Confucian gentleman-scholar. This doesn't surprise me, considering his linguistic aptitude and all the time he spent as a boy reading classic Chinese texts. Even to my untrained eye, the quick and elegant strokes of his calligraphy reveal just how supple a material this language was in his hands. I imagine Baba took great pride in his talent. I wonder, then, why he never insisted that *I* be able to read the Chinese canon—alas, that I be able to read even a Chinese menu.

Over the years, my knowledge of Chinese has ebbed and flowed; at its highest tides, it has never been more than shallow. At home, my parents communicated with each other almost entirely in Chinese, but they spoke to me in an amalgam that was maybe two-thirds Chinese, and I replied almost entirely in English. From second to seventh grade, I went to Chinese school every Sunday afternoon. But the program ended after seventh grade, and I made little effort to keep up my studies. When I got to college, I took two years of intensive Chinese to replenish my knowledge from grade school. But then I graduated, and I haven't studied Chinese since.

Not once during the ebb periods did my father ever pressure me to become more fluent. There was one time he sent me a letter in Chinese, and I thought it might be a solemn message about the importance of preserving my heritage. It turned out to be a gag, a string of silly Chinese puns. This, it seemed, was his attitude toward my dissipating Chineseness: studied nonchalance. Whenever my grandmother called us from Taiwan, I'd stumble through a few pleasantries in fractured Mandarin, and Baba would feel obliged to offer a half-serious apology for my pitiful performance. After hanging up, though, he'd never say a word to me about it.

I wish he had. Today, I am far from bilingual. In written Chinese, I am functionally illiterate; in spoken Chinese, I am 1.5-lingual at best, more suited to following conversations than joining them. True, some of the things that come hardest to non-native Mandarin speakers—an ear for the four different tones, the ability to form certain sounds—come easily to me, because I've heard the language all my life. I also, as a result, have an instinctive feel for the proper construction of Chinese sentences. What I don't have, alas, is much of a vocabulary. I can sense that thinking in Chinese yields a unique, ineffable way of perceiving the world. I can sense how useful Chinese is for filling the interstitial spaces of English. But I sense these things and express them only as a child might, since I have, really, only a child's mastery of Chinese.

When I contrast my father's possession of English with my forfeiture of Chinese, I feel like something of a fool: as if I had squandered an inheritance and not even realized its magnitude until I was left with only spare change. Yet I know that in a fundamental way it was my father's possession of English that had made possible my forfeiture of Chinese. You could say, indeed, that I merely completed his assimilation. He might have preferred deep down that I be literate in his first language. But he preferred above all that I have unimpeded access to every avenue of American life. So long as I appeared to have that, any Chinese I might have was just a bonus.

I understand this attitude, even if I regret some of its consequences now. I recognize, as well, what a luxury it is to express such regret. As he made his way in this country, my father piled up more misgivings than I may ever know. Yet he could only file them away: there was no time for such indulgences; no reason to do an honest accounting of his losses and gains. Now I attempt such an accounting. And I find myself perhaps too willing to extend the lines of the ledger: to count the first quarter of my own life as the fifth quarter of his.

Baba would not have expected, or even wanted, such a grace period. If there was one dominant theme in his life, it was that he didn't want to be treated differently—better or worse—just because he was different. This principle, and the pride that upheld it, made for a selective kind of assimilation. He did not want to be a square peg in a round hole. But he realized at a certain point that, like a chopstick, he had both a square end and a round end; that he could find ways to fit in without whittling down his integrity.

What he did with his name is a good example. Unlike some of his Chinese immigrant peers, my father never took on an "American" first name like Charlie or Chet. His concession to convention was to shorten "Chao-hua" to "Chao" and to pronounce his surname as *loo* instead of *leeoo*—so that to the white world, he was, phonetically, *chow loo*. I suppose that still sounds pretty foreign to many people (including his own mother). But by carrying himself as if the name "Chao Liu" was as American as "Chuck Lewis," he managed, in effect, to make it so.

How did he carry himself? My father had several roles when he was in public, by which I mean, in mostly white environments. One was the savvy manager. As he climbed the ranks of middle management at IBM, Dad became ever more adept at the intangibles of corporate life—the ability to read people and play internecine politics; to conform and yet distinguish himself. He knew how the system worked: knew it well enough to become one of the few Chinese faces in the upper tiers of IBM's Poughkeepsie operation; knew it well enough also to sense the leveling of his trajectory during his last years. At dinner, he and Mom would spend what seemed like hours deconstructing the latest office maneuverings, mixing gossipy news of intrigue with bits of bureaucratese. As Andrea and I sat there, bored by the grown-up talk, Dad would suddenly break out of Chinese and toss an observation our way: " 'A' students end up working for 'C' students." And then back to Chinese.

Another role he took on, probably not unrelated, was that of the pushy underdog. Dad didn't have a chip on his shoulder; he was good-natured, didn't play the victim. But in the many small transactions of our daily lives—with mechanics, teachers, salesmen, doctors, repairmen, and any other figures who might hold momentary leverage over us—Dad *was not* going to be taken advantage of. He wasn't shy about asking for documentation, explanation, and the fine print. He had no qualms about being assertive in defense of household interests. Sometimes his willingness to get in people's faces would embarrass me. Other times, I'll admit, it delighted me.

I remember being awed by Baba whenever he and Mom hosted parties for our neighbors. On those occasions he was the social dynamo: outgoing, loud, backslapping, playful. In conversation, he had a bantam energy and a penchant for running jokes that simultaneously charmed his guests and kept them from getting too personal. Every few minutes, it seemed, his high-pitched laugh would rip through the house, followed, like a wave, by the louder, more resonant guffaws of Jim, Gil,

Jack, and the other big white guys he was leaning into. What were they talking about? Sports? Neighborhood scuttlebutt? Off-color jokes? I didn't know; I knew only how exciting it was to see Dad in action.

To be sure, my father was just as energetic and jocular at all-Chinese parties. That was simply his personality. But I'd never seen a Chinese immigrant of his generation behave so exuberantly with white folks. In the presence of *yangren* ("foreigners"), most of my parents' Chinese friends, whether or not they were naturally gregarious, became more reserved and formal. As they switched to English, their guard went up. Baba's expressiveness, his bouncy self-assurance, was quite a contrast.

Of course, in the quarters of his private self, there was more to my father, more than even his own son knew. There was the same geniality and humor that he showed in public. But there was also subtlety, in the thoughtful way he gave me advice. There was gentleness, in the way he would come into my room after I'd fallen asleep to close the window and kiss me by the ear. There was an agility of spirit, in the way he happily dropped the work he was doing when Mom called him to the porch one summer evening: "Come see the moon!" They sat there, smiling and talking, while my sister and I rode our bikes past. There was grace, in the way he and Mom danced to "Hooked on Classics" on the linoleum kitchen floor. There was an omnivorous intellect that won him the family sobriquet of Walking Encyclopedia. There was ambition, impatience:

23

he'd started a doctorate, then abandoned it. There was also, in my father, an inner turmoil that revealed itself only in his fitful, twitchy naps. There was a pensiveness that would bring him into the study on Sunday afternoons just to sit by the window, rub his eyes, and smoke a cigarette. There was sadness, I now realize, a deep and silent current of existential sadness.

About a year after his death, I tried on one of the casual blazers Baba had owned, a tan Haggar herringbone. It didn't quite fit me, which I knew would be the case, but which disappointed me nonetheless. As I took it off, I found two sheets of paper folded in the interior pocket that made me think suddenly, and sharply, about my father's interior life. Scribbled on one sheet, in his distinctive hand, were the lyrics from a mournful Hank Williams ballad he used to listen to: "I'm so lonesome I could cry." On the other sheet were some notes to himself, meditations in a dense Chinese scrawl. I wondered: What do those Chinese notes say? Why did he carry this song with him? Why, to the end, did he hold it so close?

5.

In the summer of 1977, "the Liu's family," as Dad called us, took a weeklong trip to Ocean City, New Jersey. Mom had researched and planned the trip months in advance. We rented a modest "cottage," a converted garage with a kitchen, that was a few blocks from the boardwalk. After spending the day on the beach, we'd come back to the cottage for dinner. My mother, to save money, had prepared a cooler full of fruit and Chinese food. We'd eat, talk, putter around, and then Andrea and I would fall asleep with our stuffed animals on the foldout bed. Early one morning, we awakened to the strange, plaintive cry of a man walking down the boardwalk, a faraway cry that sounded to my parents like "Sweeeet-heart," and to us kids like "Sweeeet Tarts."

I will always think of that trip as a time of pure, boundless joy. I was nine. This was our first family vacation, our first six-hour drive, the first time I had ever touched and smelled the sea. My mother's recollections are more bittersweet. Just a few weeks before we were to leave, my father was informed that he was ill, life-threateningly ill, and that he would have to begin treatments immediately. He and Mom decided to go ahead with the vacation. But while my sister and I ate cotton candy and collected shells those endless August afternoons, they knew that life would be changed forever come September.

At least a year before that trip, Baba had begun to suffer wrenching headaches and fatigue, which he attributed to the stress of work. It got so bad that he would come home at lunchtime just to lie down for an hour. When finally he went to the doctor, the news could not have been more stunning: the cause of his symptoms was kidney failure, or, technically, end-stage renal disease. The doctors speculated that medication he'd taken in China as a child had damaged his kidneys, but they couldn't be sure. Now the deterioration was beyond repair. His body was no longer capable of cleansing itself. His blood was choking on its own pollutants.

I can't point now to a single moment when I realized that my father was sick. I remember that at a certain juncture that fall Dad started taking trips to the hospital in Westchester County, about an hour away, to begin dialysis treatments. He and Mom must have explained to me what was going on, because I also remember going to the hospital with them one cloudy day to behold the bulky, squat artificial-kidney machine with its dials and switches arrayed in something like a face. Having just seen *Star Wars*, I called it R2D2. The doctor laughed, my parents smiled.

Yet I don't remember now how Dad reacted to his diagnosis. Was it despair, resolve, denial? I don't remember when Dad asked that his sickness remain a family secret, though I do remember feeling we had taken a sacred vow of silence. We kept that vow, all of us, until his death. I don't remember when Dad decided he wanted to switch to home dialysis. (We kept the machine hidden in a closet.) I don't remember whether Mom had reservations about taking on the risks, the responsibility. I can only see how nervous she was the first time she helped hook him up to the machine at home. Was I scared that day? I don't remember.

I think my father would be glad to know that I don't remember these things. He tried to shield my sister and me from the pain of his sickness—not the physical pain, which he would sometimes express, but the psychic pain, which he shared only with Mom. He did so, it now seems, for his own sake as much as ours. He was too proud to be incapacitated, too private to reveal his infirmity. He could not imagine letting a disease break his stride; amazingly, it hardly did. He went about the business of his daily life, going to the office, mowing the lawn, fixing up the house, playing catch, helping us with homework, shopping for groceries, as if nothing were wrong.

Baba did not want to be treated differently for being sick. He thought his coworkers and bosses and friends and neighbors would smother him with patronizing concern, and from this belief spilled an ink-dark secrecy. We couldn't tell anyone. This was why Dad went to the hospital in Westchester: so nobody local would know. It's why we had a code word for the kidney machine: so we wouldn't give Dad away.

The rest of us swallowed the illogic whole. This was what Baba wanted, after all, what he had asked of us. It didn't feel like he was controlling us or even really imposing on us. Never did I think to ask him: What's the worst thing that would happen if people found out? Wouldn't people understand? Why do you think your place in the world is so tenuous? Instead, secrecy became the warp and woof of our family life. We became adept at making excuses for the fact that Mom and Dad were occupied and our house off-limits so much of the time. We learned to have plausible explanations always at the ready. On a few occasions we had to contort ourselves to keep the truth from observant friends. Yet after a while it all became unremarkable: the sickness, the silence that surrounded it, and the silence that surrounded the silence.

Every family has its own culture, and ours, in many ways, was characteristically Chinese American: stir-fried flavors, invented traditions, inside jokes in a hybrid tongue. But our family culture also included this: The pulse and hum of the kidney machine, as it pumped my father's blood through a filter three nights a week, five hours a night. Quarterly trips to the shipping depot across the river to pick up boxes of artificial-kidney devices, saline solution, Betadine, tubes, pads, tape, and other supplies, then bring them back, unload them into the basement, and crush the dozens of empty boxes that had molded and sagged there. Long-sleeved shirts for Dad, even in summer, to hide the scabrous fistula and needle wounds in his left forearm. The habit of keeping half an ear open at all times for the sudden, grating alarm that the machine would sound if something in Dad's blood chemistry was off. Being asked by Mom to pray, though I'd never known how to pray, when Dad was hospitalized for one of several episodes of pneumonia. Incorporating those superficially Christian prayers into the intricate, many-tiered complex of superstitions I had erected to ward off further calamity.

The stereotype holds that the Chinese mind is clannish, suspicious, haunted, obsessed with face. And in the way we responded to my father's situation perhaps my family fit the

stereotype. We were insular and secretive, sometimes pro-
foundly irrational. Anxieties that could not be named circled
us like ghosts. We fashioned an elaborate front, and behind
that front there was often sorrow and foreboding. But the truth
is, there was also happiness—a true and tender happiness. In
our self-enclosed domain, we came to forget the fundamental
troubles. We forgot about things like mortality, things that
might make the latticework of our existence seem unbearably
fragile. We did not record the past or prepare for the worst.
Instead, we lived the unknowing bliss of the moment. Was this
typically Chinese? Or was it, rather, typically American?

For a while I had a theory that my father's actions, on some
level, had been motivated by the dread of racial stigma. I con-
jectured that his secrecy, far from being "typically Chinese"
behavior, was actually a preemptive strike against *anti-Chinese*
behavior: a way to fit in, to hide his difference, to insure against
mistreatment. But my mother dismissed the notion. Dad
wasn't a fearful victim, she said. And this wasn't about the fear
of racial discrimination. After all, he had concealed the facts
from *Chinese* friends as well. His only sin was that he was too
proud to let others know he was sick.

I realized, as Mom insisted on this, that it was I, not my
father, who had conflated the desire to hide the disease with
the desire to downplay difference of another kind. It was I, not
my father, who had boxed against the shame and shadow of
racial stigma. I had my own set of reasons for going along with

the family charade: as a Chinese boy in an American world, I wanted generally to project a *normal* image, to cloak any handicap, real or imagined. As a Chinese boy in an American world, I was accustomed to façades.

I wish I knew what Dad thought. I have, in so many ways, learned from my father: learned to be assertive, to be kind, to disarm with charm. Also: to be mindful of appearances, to keep things in the family, to never depend on the kindness of others. I learned how to live only in the present. This I learned perhaps too well. For so much of my inheritance today seems depthless and desultory. Where my father disdained cheap emotions, I deal in nostalgia and sugary sentimentality. Where my father knew how to salvage dignity from great dreams that had been eaten away, I have mainly a talent for mythmaking. Where my father seemed to have an endless reserve of inner strength and self-knowledge, I have but an echoing well.

To fill the hollow, I look sometimes to Chineseness. Where does my Chineseness lie? In my looks, surely. In my culture, vestigially. In my behavior, too? I have been told, in the years since my father died, that I have been the prototypical Confucian son, a textbook example of filial loyalty to my mother. But if that is true, is it because Chinese values seeped down into me? Or is it because I am the first child and only son of a widow, whom I love, who has become perhaps my closest friend? I find it difficult to separate out the part of my behavior shaped by ethnicity and the part shaped by my situation. I also find it, after a while, pointless. The longer I stare in the mirror, looking for telltale evidence of Chineseness behind the epicanthic fold of the eye, the more I suspect that the truth is to be found in my peripheral field of vision.

What is Chineseness? It is anything, everything, and ultimately nothing. In the end, Chineseness does nothing to explain the courage my father summoned to endure fourteen years of dialysis, more years than the doctors had ever thought possible. It does nothing to explain the horror, the all-consuming vacuum of his sudden, unexpected death in the middle of what seemed like a manageable bout of infection. Nor does it explain my mother's determination, in the aftermath, to face herself and "to experience life," as she says, without illusion. It does nothing, for the Liu's family, to ease the phantom pain of our missing limb—or to explain why, despite the pain, I can still giggle out loud at the mere thought of Baba. When your father, who was Chinese, has died, Chineseness seems an irrelevance: an inert container, just one among many, for holding the memories of shared experience. When your father has died, you realize this: it is the liquid of memory, not the cup we drink it from, that gives our lives content and reveals our humanity.

The last time I saw my father before the weekend he died, we were on our way home together. It was the Friday before Memorial Day. He was on assignment in New York City, I was coming up from Washington, and we decided to meet in Manhattan and then take the commuter train back to Poughkeep-sie. It was a windy day, and we met at a new Chinese noodle shop near his office. Baba took obvious ethnic pride in this small shop: it was clean, modern, bustling, efficient, and served huge steaming bowls of spicy noodle soup for what seemed a pittance. Our conversation was animated. I remember, in this restaurant, slipping into Chinese more freely. As I sat across a small table from my father, I thought to myself, this is our future: Dad had just begun an exciting new job, I was a year into my postgraduate life in politics. We ate heartily, even sloppily. When we stepped out of the shop, the wind had picked up and the skies were churning. We caught a cab just before the rain arrived.

Sometimes I'll think of that afternoon, or think of all that my father and I imagined doing together, or think of something he once said to me, or look into a photograph of him, or wonder what he would think of the person I have become, and I'll lose myself in reminiscence, straining to recall the timbre of his voice, the arpeggio of his laughter, the sound of his sleep, and before I even realize that I have opened my mouth and drawn a breath, I will hear the word float off my lips: "Baba?"

Notes
of a
Native
Speaker

1.

Here are some of the ways you could say I am "white":

I listen to National Public Radio.
I wear khaki Dockers.
I own brown suede bucks.
I eat gourmet greens.
I have few close friends "of color."
I married a white woman.
I am a child of the suburbs.
I furnish my condo à la Crate & Barrel.
I vacation in charming bed-and-breakfasts.
I have never once been the victim of blatant discrimination.
I am a member of several exclusive institutions.

I have been in the inner sanctums of political power.

I have been there as something other than an attendant.

I have the ambition to return.

I am a producer of the culture.

I expect my voice to be heard.

I speak flawless, unaccented English.

I subscribe to *Foreign Affairs*.

I do not mind when editorialists write in the first person plural.

I do not mind how white television casts are.

I am not too ethnic.

I am wary of minority militants.

I consider myself neither in exile nor in opposition.

I am considered "a credit to my race."

I never asked to be white. I am not literally white. That is, I do not have white skin or white ancestors. I have yellow skin and yellow ancestors, hundreds of generations of them. But like so many other Asian Americans of the second generation, I find myself now the bearer of a strange new status: white, by acclamation. Thus it is that I have been described as an "honorary white," by other whites, and as a "banana," by other Asians. Both the honorific and the epithet take as a given this idea: to the extent that I have moved away from the periphery and toward the center of American life, I have become white inside. *Some are born white, others achieve whiteness, still others have whiteness thrust upon them.* This, supposedly, is what it means to assimilate.

There was a time when assimilation did quite strictly mean whitening. In fact, well into the first half of this century, mimicry of the stylized standards of the WASP gentry was the proper, dominant, perhaps even sole method of ensuring that your origins would not be held against you. You "made it" in society not only by putting on airs of anglitude, but also by assiduously bleaching out the marks of a darker, dirtier past. And this bargain, stifling as it was, was open to European immigrants almost exclusively; to blacks, only on the passing occasion; to Asians, hardly at all.

Times have changed, and I suppose you could call it progress that a Chinaman, too, may now aspire to whiteness. But precisely because the times have changed, that aspiration—and the *imputation* of the aspiration—now seems astonishingly outmoded. The meaning of "American" has undergone a revolution in the twenty-nine years I have been alive, a revolution of color, class, and culture. Yet the vocabulary of "assimilation" has remained fixed all this time: fixed in whiteness, which is still our metonym for power; and fixed in shame, which is what the colored are expected to feel for embracing the power.

I have assimilated. I am of the mainstream. In many ways I fit the psychological profile of the so-called banana: imitative, impressionable, rootless, eager to please. As I will admit in this essay, I have at times gone to great lengths to downplay my difference, the better to penetrate the "establishment" of the moment. Yet I'm not sure that what I did was so cut-and-dried as "becoming white." I plead guilty to the charges above: achieving, learning the ways of the upper middle class, distancing myself from radicals of any hue. But having confessed, I still do not know my crime.

To be an accused banana is to stand at the ill-fated intersection of class and race. And because class is the only thing Americans have more trouble talking about than race, a minority's climb up the social ladder is often willfully misnamed and wrongly portrayed. There is usually, in the portrayal, a strong whiff of betrayal: the assimilist is a traitor to his kind, to his class, to his own family. He cannot gain the world without losing his soul. To be sure, something *is* lost in any migration, whether from place to place or from class to class. But something is gained as well. And the result is always more complicated than the monochrome language of "whiteness" and "authenticity" would suggest.

My own assimilation began long before I was born. It began with my parents, who came here with an appetite for Western ways already whetted by films and books and music and, in my mother's case, by a father who'd been to the West. My parents, who traded Chinese formality for the more laissez-faire stance of this country. Who made their way by hard work and quiet adaptation. Who fashioned a comfortable life in a quiet development in a second-tier suburb. Who, unlike your "typical" Chinese parents, were not pushy, status-obsessed, rigid, disciplined, or prepared. Who were haphazard about passing down ancestral traditions and "lessons" to their children. Who did pass down, however, the sense that their children were entitled to mix and match, as they saw fit, whatever aspects of whatever cultures they encountered.

I was raised, in short, to assimilate, to claim this place as mine. I don't mean that my parents told me to act like an American. That's partly the point: they didn't tell me to do anything except to be a good boy. They trusted I would find my way, and I did, following their example and navigating by the lights of the culture that encircled me like a dome. As a function of my parents' own half-conscious, half-finished acculturation, I grew up feeling that my life was Book II of an ongoing saga. Or that I was running the second leg of a relay race. *Slap!* I was out of the womb and sprinting, baton in hand. Gradually more sure of my stride, my breathing, the feel of the track beneath me. Eyes forward, never backward.

Today, nearly seven years after my father's death and two years after my marriage into a large white family, it is as if I have come round a bend and realized that I am no longer sure where I am running or why. My sprint slows to a trot. I scan the unfamiliar vista that is opening up. I am somewhere else now, somewhere far from the China that yielded my mother and father; far, as well, from the modest horizons I knew as a boy. I look at my limbs and realize I am no longer that boy; my gait and grasp exceed his by an order of magnitude. Now I want desperately to see my face, to see what time has marked and what it has erased. But I can find no mirror except the people who surround me. And they are mainly pale, powerful.

How did I end up here, standing in what seems the very seat of whiteness, gazing from the promontory of social privilege? How did I cover so much ground so quickly? What was it, in my blind journey, that I felt I should leave behind? And what *did* I leave behind? This, the jettisoning of one mode of life to send another aloft, is not only the immigrant's tale; it is the son's tale, too. By coming to America, my parents made themselves into citizens of a new country. By traveling the trajectory of an assimilist, so did I.

2.

As a child, I lived in a state of "amoebic bliss," to borrow the felicitous phrase of the author of *Nisei Daughter*, Monica Sone. The world was a gossamer web of wonder that began with life at home, extended to my friendships, and made the imaginary realm of daydream seem as immediate as the real. If something or someone was in my personal web of meaning, then color or station was irrelevant. I made no distinctions in fourth grade between my best friend, a black boy named Kimathi, and my next-best friend, a white boy named

Charlie—other than the fact that one was number one, the other number two. I did not feel, or feel for, a seam that separated the textures of my Chinese life from those of my American life. I was not "bicultural" but omnicultural, and omnivorous, too. To my mind, I differed from others in only two ways that counted: I was a faster runner than most, and a better student. Thus did work blend happily with play, school with home, Western culture with Eastern: it was all the same to a self-confident boy who believed he'd always be at the center of his own universe.

As I approached adolescence, though, things shifted. Suddenly, I could no longer subsume the public world under my private concept of self. Suddenly, the public world was more complicated than just a parade of smiling teachers and a few affirming friends. Now I had to contend with the unstated, inchoate, but inescapable standards of *cool*. The essence of cool was the ability to conform. The essence of conformity was the ability to anticipate what was cool. And I wasn't so good at that. For the first time, I had found something that did not come effortlessly to me. No one had warned me about this transition from happy amoeboid to social animal; no one had prepared me for the great labors of fitting in.

And so in three adjoining arenas—my looks, my loves, my manners—I suffered a bruising adolescent education. I don't mean to overdramatize: there was, in these teenage banalities, usually something humorous and nothing particularly tragic.

But in each of these realms, I came to feel I was not normal. And obtusely, I ascribed the difficulties of that age not to my age but to my color. I came to suspect that there was an order to things, an order that I, as someone Chinese, could perceive but not quite crack. I responded not by exploding in rebellion but by dedicating myself, quietly and sometimes angrily, to learning the order as best I could. I was never ashamed of being Chinese; I was, in fact, rather proud to be linked to a great civilization. But I was mad that my difference should matter now. And if it had to matter, I did not want it to defeat me.

Consider, if you will, my hair. For the first eleven years of my life, I sported what was essentially the same hairstyle: a tapered bowl cut, the handiwork of my mother. For those eleven joyful years, this low-maintenance do was entirely satisfactory. But in my twelfth year, as sixth grade got under way, I became aware—gradually at first, then urgently—that bangs were no longer the look for boys. This was the year when certain early bloomers first made the height-weight-physique distribution in our class seem startlingly wide—and when I first realized that I was lingering near the bottom. It was essential that I compensate for my childlike mien by cultivating at least a patina of teenage style.

This is where my hair betrayed me. For some readers the words "Chinese hair" should suffice as explanation. For the rest, particularly those who have spent all your lives with the ability to comb back, style, and part your hair *at will*, what follows should make you count your blessings. As you may recall, 1980 was a vintage year for hair that was parted straight down the middle, then feathered on each side, feathered so immaculately that the ends would meet in the back like the closed wings of angels. I dreamed of such hair. I imagined tossing my head back casually, to ease into place the one or two strands that had drifted from their positions. I dreamed of wearing the fluffy, tailored locks of the blessed.

Instead, I was cursed. My hair was straight, rigid, and wiry. Not only did it fail to feather back; it would not even bend. Worse still, it grew the wrong way. That is, it all emanated from a single swirl near the rear edge of my scalp. Parting my hair in any direction except back to front, the way certain balding men stage their final retreat, was a physical impossibility. It should go without saying that this was a disaster. For the next three years, I experimented with a variety of hairstyles that ranged from the ridiculous to the sublimely bad. There was the stringy pothead look. The mushroom do. Helmet head. Bangs folded back like curtains. I enlisted a blow-dryer, a Conair set on high heat, to force my hair into stiff postures of submission. The results, though sometimes innovative, fell always far short of cool.

I feigned nonchalance, and no one ever said anything about it. But make no mistake: this was one of the most consuming crises of my inner life as a young teen. Though neither of my parents had ever had such troubles, I blamed this predicament squarely on my Chinese genes. And I could not abide my fate. At a time when homogeneity was the highest virtue, I felt I stood out like a pigtailed Manchu.

My salvation didn't come until the end of junior high, when one of my buddies, in an epiphany as we walked past the Palace of Hair Design, dared me to get my head shaved. Without hesitation, I did it—to the tearful laughter of my friends and, soon afterward, the tearful horror of my mother. Of course, I had moments of doubt the next few days as I rubbed my peach-fuzzed skull. But what I liked was this: I had managed, without losing face, to rid myself of my greatest social burden. What's more, in the eyes of some classmates, I was now a bold (if bald) iconoclast. I've worn a crew cut ever since.

Well-styled hair was only one part of a much larger preoccupation during the ensuing years: wooing girls. In this realm I experienced a most frustrating kind of success. I was the boy that girls always found "sweet" and "funny" and "smart" and "nice." Which, to my highly sensitive ear, sounded like "leprous." Time and again, I would charm a girl into deep friendship. Time and again, as the possibility of romance came within reach, I would smash into what I took to be a glass ceiling.

The girls were white, you see; such were the demographics of my school. I was Chinese. And I was convinced that this was the sole obstacle to my advancement. It made sense, did it not? I was, after all, sweet and funny and smart and nice. Hair notwithstanding, I was not unattractive, at least compared with some of the beasts who had started "going out" with girls. There was simply no other explanation. Yet I could never say this out loud: it would have been the whining of a loser. My response, then, was to secretly scorn the girls I coveted. It was *they* who were subpar, whose small-mindedness and veiled prejudice made them unworthy.

My response, too, was to take refuge in my talents. I made myself into a Renaissance boy, playing in the orchestra but also joining the wrestling team, winning science prizes but also editing the school paper. I thought I was defying the stereotype of the Asian American male as a one-dimensional nerd. But in the eyes of some, I suppose, I was simply another "Asian over-achiever."

In hindsight, it's hard to know exactly how great a romantic penalty I paid for being Chinese. There may have been girls who would have had nothing to do with me on account of my race, but I never knew them. There were probably girls who, race aside, simply didn't like me. And then there were girls who liked me well enough but who also shied from the prospect of being part of an interracial couple. With so many boys out there, they probably reasoned, why take the path of greater resistance? Why risk so many status points? Why not be "just friends" with this Chinese boy?

Maybe this stigma was more imagined than real. But being an ABC ("American-born Chinese," as our parents called us) certainly affected me another way. It made me feel like something of a greenhorn, a social immigrant. I wanted so greatly to be liked. And my earnestness, though endearing, was not the sort of demeanor that won girls' hearts. Though I was observant enough to notice how people talked when flirting, astute enough to mimic the forms, I was oblivious to the subterranean levels of courtship, blind to the more subtle rituals of "getting chicks" by spurning them. I held the view that if you were manifestly a good person, eventually someone of the opposite sex would do the rational thing and be smitten with you. I was clueless. Many years would pass before I'd wise up.

It wasn't just dating rituals that befuddled me as a youth. It was ritual of all kinds. Ceremony, protocol, etiquette—all these made me feel like an awkward stranger. Things that came as second nature to many white kids were utterly exotic to me. American-style manners, for instance. Chinese families often have their own elaborate etiquette, but "please" and "may I" weren't the sort of words ever heard around my house. That kind of formality seemed so beside the point. I was never taught by my parents to write thank-you notes. I didn't even have the breeding to *say* "Thank you" after sleeping over at a friend's house. I can recall the awful, sour feeling in my stomach when this friend told me his mother had been offended by my impoliteness. (At that point, I expressed my thanks.)

Eating dinner at the home of a *yangren* could be especially trying. The oaken furniture seemed scaled-up, chairs like thrones. The meal would begin with someone, usually the father, mumbling grace. Furtively, I'd steal a glance at the heads bowed in prayer. What if they asked me to say something? I looked back down and kept my mouth shut. Next was the question of silverware: which pieces to use, in which order, and so forth. I'd realize then that at home I ate by using chopsticks to shove rice and meat straight from bowl to slurping mouth. Then the whole thing about passing platters of food around the table, instead of just reaching over and getting what you wanted. I would hear myself ask, in too-high tones, "Would you please pass the carrots, please?" It was usually at that point that I would notice that my napkin was the only one still folded neatly on the table.

All this, of course, was in the context of being with my friends and having a nice time. But something made me feel vaguely sad while I sat there, swallowing huge servings of gravy-drenched food with this other family. These were the moments when I realized I was becoming something other than my parents. I wanted so badly then just to be home, in my own kitchen, taking in the aroma of stir-fry on the wok and the chattery sounds of Chinglish. And yet, like an amphibian that has just breached the shore, I could not stop inhaling this wondrous new atmosphere. My moist, blinking eyes opened wide, observing and recording the customs and predilections of these "regular" Americans. The more time I spent in their midst, the more I learned to be like them. To make their everyday idioms and idiosyncrasies familiar. To possess them.

This, the mundane, would be the locus of my conversion. It was through the small things that I made myself over. I wish, if only for storytelling purposes, that I could offer a more dramatic tale, a searing incident of racism that sent me into deep, self-abnegating alienation. The truth is, I can't. I was sometimes uncomfortable, but never really alienated. There were one or two occasions in seventh grade when the toughs in the back of the bus taunted me, called me *chink*, shot spitballs at me. I didn't like it. But each time, one of my friends—one of my white friends, in whose house I'd later eat dinner—would stand with me and fire back both spitballs and insults. Our insults were mean, too: scornful references to the trailer parks where these kids lived or the grubby clothes they wore or the crummy jobs their parents had. These skirmishes weren't just about race; they were also about mobility.

The same could be said, ultimately, about my own assimilation. To say simply that I became a banana, that I became white-identified, is somewhat simplistic. As an impressionable teen, I came to identify not with white people in general but with that subset of people, most of them white, who were educated, affluent: *going places.* It was their cues that I picked up, their judgments that I cared about. It was in their presence that old patterns of thought began to fall away like so much scaffolding around my psyche. It was in their presence that I began to imagine myself beyond race.

3.

I recently dug up a photograph of myself from freshman year of college that made me smile. I have on the wrong shoes, the wrong socks, the wrong checkered shirt tucked the wrong way into the wrong slacks. I look like what I was: a boy sprung from a middlebrow burg who affected a secondhand preppiness. I look nervous. Compare that image to one from my senior-class dinner: now I am attired in a gray tweed jacket with a green plaid bow tie and a sensible button-down shirt, all purchased at the Yale Co-op. I look confident, and more than a bit contrived.

What happened in between those two photographs is that I experienced, then overcame, what the poet Meena Alexander has called "the shock of arrival." When I was deposited at the wrought-iron gates of my residential college as a freshman, I felt more like an outsider than I'd thought possible. It wasn't just that I was a small Chinese boy standing at a grand WASP temple; nor simply that I was a hayseed neophyte puzzled by the refinements of college style. It was *both*: color and class were all twisted together in a double helix of felt inadequacy.

For a while I coped with the shock by retreating to a group of my own kind—not fellow Asians, but fellow marginal public-school grads who resented the rah-rah Yalies to whom everything came so effortlessly. Aligning myself this way was bearable—I was hiding, but at least I could place myself in a long tradition of underdog exiles at Yale. Aligning myself by race, on the other hand, would have seemed too inhibiting.

I know this doesn't make much sense. I know also that college, in the multicultural era, is supposed to be where the deracinated minority youth discovers the "person of color" inside. To a point, I did. I studied Chinese, took an Asian American history course, a seminar on race politics. But ultimately, college was where the unconscious habits of my adolescent assimilation hardened into self-conscious strategy.

I still remember the moment, in the first week of school, when I came upon a table in Yale Station set up by the Asian American Student Association. The upperclassman staffing the table was pleasant enough. He certainly did not strike me as a fanatic. Yet, for some reason, I flashed immediately to a scene I'd witnessed days earlier, on the corner outside. Several Lubavitcher Jews, dressed in black, their faces bracketed by dangling side curls, were looking for fellow travelers at this busy crossroads. Their method was crude but memorable. As any vaguely Jewish-looking male walked past, the zealots would quickly approach, extend a pamphlet, and ask, "Excuse me, sir, are you Jewish?" Since most were not, and since those who were weren't about to stop, the result was a frantic, nervous, almost comical buzz all about the corner: Excuse me, are you Jewish? Are you Jewish? Excuse me. Are you Jewish?

I looked now at the clean-cut Korean boy at the AASA table (I think I can distinguish among Asian ethnicities as readily as those Hasidim thought they could tell Gentile from Jew), and though he had merely offered an introductory hello and was now smiling mutely at me, in the back of my mind I heard only this: *Excuse me, are you Asian? Are you Asian? Excuse me. Are you Asian?* I took one of the flyers on the table, even put my name on a mailing list, so as not to appear impolite. But I had already resolved not to be active in any Asians-only group. I thought then: I would never *choose* to be so pigeonholed.

This allergic sensitivity to "pigeonholing" is one of the unhappy hallmarks of the banana mentality. What does the banana fear? That is, what did *I* fear? The possibility of being mistaken for someone more Chinese. The possibility of being known only, or even primarily, for being Asian. The possibility of being written off by whites as a self-segregating ethnic clumper. These were the threats—unseen and, frankly, unsub-stantiated—that I felt I should keep at bay.

I didn't avoid making Asian friends in college or working with Asian classmates; I simply never went out of my way to do so. This distinction seemed important—it marked, to my mind, the difference between self-hate and self-respect. That the two should have been so proximate in the first place never struck me as odd, or telling. Nor did it ever occur to me that the reasons I gave myself for dissociating from Asians as a group—that I didn't want to be part of a clique, that I didn't want to get absorbed and lose my individuality—were the very developments that marked my own assimilation. I simply hewed to my ideology of race neutrality and self-reliance. I didn't need that crutch, I told myself nervously, that crutch of racial affinity. What's more, I was vaguely insulted by the presumption that I might.

But again: Who was making the presumption? Who more than I was taking the mere existence of Korean volleyball leagues or Taiwanese social sets or pan-Asian student clubs to mean that *all* people of Asian descent, myself included, needed such quasi-kinship groups? And who more than I interpreted this need as infirmity, as a failure to fit in? I resented the faintly sneering way that some whites regarded Asians as an undifferentiated mass. But whose sneer, really, did I resent more than my own?

I was keenly aware of the unflattering mythologies that attach to Asian Americans: that we are indelibly foreign, exotic, math and science geeks, numbers people rather than people people, followers and not leaders, physically frail but devious and sneaky, unknowable and potentially treacherous. These stereotypes of Asian otherness and inferiority were like immense blocks of ice sitting before me, challenging me to chip away at them. And I did, tirelessly. All the while, though, I was oblivious to rumors of my *own* otherness and inferiority, rumors that rose off those blocks like a fog, wafting into my consciousness and chilling my sense of self.

As I had done in high school, I combated the stereotypes in part by trying to disprove them. If Asians were reputed to be math and science geeks, I would be a student of history and politics. If Asians were supposed to be feeble subalterns, I'd lift weights and go to Marine officer candidate school. If Asians were alien, I'd be ardently patriotic. If Asians were shy and retiring, I'd try to be exuberant and jocular. If they were narrow-minded specialists, I'd be a well-rounded generalist. If they were perpetual outsiders, I'd join every establishment outfit I could and show that I, too, could run with the swift.

I overstate, of course. It wasn't that I chose to do all these things with no other purpose than to cut against a supposed convention. I was neither so Pavlovian nor so calculating that I would simply remake myself into the opposite of what people expected. I actually *liked* history, and wasn't especially good at math. As the grandson of a military officer, I *wanted* to see what officer candidates school would be like, and I enjoyed it, at least once I'd finished. I am *by nature* enthusiastic and alle-giant, a joiner, and a bit of a jingo.

At the same time, I was often aware, sometimes even hopeful, that others might think me "exceptional" for my race. I derived satisfaction from being the "atypical" Asian, the only Chinese face at OCS or in this club or that.

The irony is that in working so duteously to defy stereotype, I became a slave to it. For to act self-consciously against Asian "tendencies" is not to break loose from the cage of myth and legend; it is to turn the very key that locks you inside. What spontaneity is there when the value of every act is measured, at least in part, by its power to refute a presumption about why you act? The *typical Asian* I imagined, and the *atypical Asian* I imagined myself to be, were identical in this sense: neither was as much a creature of free will as a human being ought to be.

Let me say it plainly, then: I am not proud to have had this mentality. I believe I have outgrown it. And I expose it now not to justify it but to detoxify it, to prevent its further spread.

Yet it would be misleading, I think, to suggest that my education centered solely on the discomfort caused by race. The fact is, when I first got to college I felt deficient compared with people of *every* color. Part of why I believed it so necessary to achieve was that I lacked the connections, the wealth, the experience, the sophistication that so many of my classmates seemed to have. I didn't get the jokes or the intellectual references. I didn't have the canny attitude. So in addition to all my coursework, I began to puzzle over this, the culture of the influential class.

Over time, I suppose, I learned the culture. My interests and vocabulary became ever more worldly. I made my way onto what Calvin Trillin once described as the "magic escalator" of a Yale education. Extracurriculars opened the door to an alumni internship, which brought me to Capitol Hill, which led to a job and a life in Washington after commencement. Gradually, very gradually, I found that I was not so much of an outsider anymore. I found that by almost any standard, but particularly by the standards of my younger self, I was actually beginning to "make it."

It has taken me until now, however, to appraise the thoughts and acts of that younger self. I can see now that the straitening path I took was not the only or even the best path. For while it may be possible to transcend race, *it is not always necessary to try.* And while racial identity is sometimes a shackle, it is not *only* a shackle. I could have spared myself a great deal of heartache had I understood this earlier, that the choice of race is not simply "embrace or efface."

I wonder sometimes how I would have turned out had I been, from the start, more comfortable in my own skin. What did I miss by distancing myself from race? What friendships did I forgo, what self-knowledge did I defer? Had certain accidents of privilege been accidents of privation or exclusion, I might well have developed a different view of the world. But I do not know just how my view would have differed.

What I know is that through all those years of shadow-dancing with my identity, something happened, something that had only partially to do with color. By the time I left Yale I was no longer the scared boy of that freshman photo. I had become more sure of myself and of my place—sure enough, indeed, to perceive the folly of my fears. And in the years since, I have assumed a sense of expectation, of access and *belonging,* that my younger self could scarcely have imagined. All this happened incrementally. There was no clear tipping point, no obvious moment of mutation. The shock of arrival, it would seem, is simply that I arrived.

4.

"The world is white no longer, and it will never be white again." So wrote James Baldwin after having lived in a tiny Swiss village where, to his knowledge, no black man had ever set foot. It was there, in the icy heart of whiteness, that the young expatriate began to comprehend the desire of so many of his countrymen to return to some state of nature where only white people existed. It was there too that he recognized just how impossible that was, just how intertwined were the fates and identities of the races in America. "No road whatever will lead Americans back to the simplicity of this European village where white men still have the luxury of looking on me as a stranger," he wrote. "I am not, really, a stranger any longer for any American alive."

That is precisely how I feel when I consider my own journey, my own family's travels. For here I am now, standing in a new country. Not as an expatriate or a resident alien, but as a citizen. And as I survey this realm—this Republic of Privilege—I realize certain things, things that my mother and father might also have realized about *their* new country a generation ago. I realize that my entry has yielded me great opportunities. I realize, as well, that my route of entry has taken a certain toll. I have neglected my ancestral heritage. I have lost something. Yes, I can speak some Mandarin and stir-fry a few easy dishes. I have been to China and know something of its history. Still, I could never claim to be Chinese at the core.

Yet neither would I claim, as if by default, to be merely "white inside." I do not want to be white. I only want to be integrated. When I identify with white people who wield economic and political power, it is not for their whiteness but for their power. When I imagine myself among white people who influence the currents of our culture, it is not for their whiteness but for their influence. When I emulate white people who are at ease with the world, it is not for their whiteness but for their ease. I don't like it that the people I should learn from tend so often to be white, for it says something damning about how opportunity is still distributed. But it helps not at all to call me white for learning from them. It is cruel enough that the least privileged Americans today have colored skin, the most privileged fair. It is crueler still that by our very language we should help convert this fact into rule. The time has come to describe assimilation as something other than the White Way of Being.

The time has also come, I think, to conceive of assimilation as more than a series of losses—and to recognize that what is lost is not necessarily sacred. I have, as I say, allowed my Chinese ethnicity to become diluted. And I often resolve to do more to preserve, to conserve, my inheritance. But have my acts of neglect thus far, my many omissions, been inherently wrong? G. K. Chesterton once wrote that "conservatism is based upon the idea that if you leave things alone, you leave them as they are. But you do not. If you leave a thing alone, you leave it to a torrent of change." I may have been born a

Chinese baby, but it would have taken unremitting reinforcement, by my parents and by myself, for me to have remained Chinese. Instead, we left things alone. And a torrent of change washed over me.

This, we must remember, has been an act of creation as much as destruction. Something new is emerging from the torrent, in my case and the many millions like it. Something undeveloped, speaking the unformed tongue of an unformed nation. Something not white, and probably more Chinese than I know. Whatever it is that I am becoming, is it any less authentic for being an amalgam? Is it intrinsically less meaningful than what I might otherwise have been? In every assimilation, there is a mutiny against history—but there is also a destiny, which is to redefine history. What it means to be American—in spirit, in blood—is something far more borrowed and commingled than anything previous generations ever knew. Alongside the pain of migration, then, and the possibility, there is this truth: America is white no longer, and it will never be white again.

The
Accidental
Asian

VARIATIONS ON A THEME

1.

The Asian American identity was born, as I was, roughly thirty years ago. In those three decades it has struggled to find relevance and a coherent voice. As I have. It has tried to adapt itself to the prevailing attitudes about race—namely, that one matters in this society, if one is colored, mainly to the extent that one claims a race for oneself. I, too, have tried to accommodate these forces. The Asian American identity, like me, renounces whiteness. It draws strength from the possibility of transcending the fear and blindness of the past. So do I. It is the so very American product of a rejection of history's limitations, rooted in little more than its own creation a generation ago. As I am.

What I am saying is that I can identify with the Asian American identity. I understand why it does what it does. It is as if this identity and I were twin siblings, separated at birth but endowed with uncanny foreknowledge of each other's motives. The problem is, I disagree with it often. I become frustrated by it, even disappointed. The feeling is mutual, I suspect. We react to the same world in very different ways.

And yes, I do think of this identity as something that reacts, something almost alive, in the way that a shadow, or a mirror image—or a conscience—is almost alive. It has, if not a will of its own, then at least a highly developed habit of asserting its existence. It is like a storm, a beautiful, swirling weather pattern that moves back and forth across my mind. It draws me in, it repulses me. I am ever aware of its presence. There is always part of me that believes I will find deliverance if I merge with this identity. Yet still I hold it at a remove. For I fear that in the middle of this swirl, this great human churn, lies emptiness.

2.

What must it be like to be told you are Asian American? Imagine that you are an immigrant, young, but old enough to get by, and you have been in America for only a few months. Imagine that you come from Korea. Imagine that you speak Korean, read Korean newspapers, eat Korean food. Imagine that you live in East Flushing or in South Central and you see only the Korean faces. There are other faces, yes, brown and black and yellow and white, but the ones you see, the ones you can read, are Korean. Imagine that time passes, and you realize now that you see the other faces. Imagine that the order of life in this city, the invisible grid, has become visible to you. More than that, it has affected you. What was Korean before is not exactly Korean anymore: your speech is interspersed now with fragments of English, Spanish; your daily paper you must find at a crowded, strange-smelling newsstand, tucked among bundles of other scripts and shades of print; your strong, salty food, supplemented now by frosted cereal and cookies, you eat while quietly absorbed by a television program you cannot understand except in mime. Imagine that you are becoming a Korean American. Is that not shock enough? To know that what was once the noun is becoming the adjective? And so perhaps you retreat, you compensate, you remind yourself every night before you pray that you are Korean so that you and your Maker will not forget. But imagine that the forgetting is relentless. That more time passes, and a knock on the door of your apartment brings you face-to-face with a Japanese, and something deep inside you, a passing sneer or a cautionary tale, a history, twinges. And imagine that this Japanese begins speaking to you in English, the kind of English the television produces, and you understand perfectly what she is saying. Imagine that what she is saying is that she needs your help. That you are invited to a rally (or is it a party?). That we—you and this Japanese and so many unseen others—must stand together against a common foe. Imagine that what she is saying is that you are Asian American. What must it be like? What do you think about when you close the door and walk to the window and realize, while peering out over a scene of so many unknowable lives but four knowable colors, how faint the aroma of your own kitchen has become, how strong the scent of the street?

3.

I find myself in a cavernous television studio, seated beside the anchorwoman. The cameras are on us, lights are burning overhead. I am nervous, although I shouldn't be: this is my job. I do commentary for a cable news network and I come to this studio often. This day, I have been called in as a "special guest" to discuss a recent and controversial cover of the *National Review* magazine depicting the president, vice president, and first lady in yellowface—that is, in stereotypical Oriental caricature. "The Manchurian Candidate," reads the cover text, referring, of course, to Bill Clinton and his role in the "Asian money" scandal that has been brewing since the 1996 election.

The news package leading up to my entrance describes the brouhaha that has arisen over the cover, and as the tape comes to a close a red light comes on, signaling that we are on the air. The anchor turns to me, her brow knit at the appropriate angle of concern: "What about this cover do you find offensive, Eric?"

Truth be told, I was not deeply offended when I first saw the cover. (My mother, in fact, was much angrier.) I mainly thought it was juvenile, sophomoric. And I didn't think about it again until a few days later, when my producer waved it at me and asked for a reaction. I knew what answer he was looking for; what answer any self-respecting Asian would give.

"Well," I say, turning now to the camera, "these caricatures play off a long history of demeaning anti-Asian stereotypes— the buckteeth, the slanted eyes, the bamboo hat. They are racist in their effect." And on I go. I play, in other words, the Asian spokesman, ever vigilant against affronts to my race. The anchor nods understandingly as I speak.

Soon a staff writer from the *Review* joins the discussion via satellite. He, too, is Asian American, South Asian. "We didn't think this cover would be particularly controversial," I hear this other Asian say. "Normal people aren't offended by it."

Normal people? The more this other Asian talks, the more heated I become in my responses. At first I assume it's the adrenaline rush of verbal combat. But as he goes on mouthing his disingenuous party line—something like, "We would've used leprechauns if this scandal was about Irish money"—I become more than just irked, more than angry, until suddenly I realize that I am outraged. I am sending a searing look into my own reflection in the camera as I argue. And I am shouting now: I have raised my voice to defend *my people.*

"Somehow, we have gotten to the point where those who protest bias and insensitivity are *demonized* more than those who commit it!" I boom.

"I'm not demonizing you," the other Asian offers.

The segment ends shortly afterward, the red light goes off. An Asian American employee comes over to shake my hand. I feel pleased with myself, pumped up. But even before I've removed my mike, I realize something unusual has happened. When the debate began I was playing a part, because I felt I should. Eight minutes later I had merged completely with my role. Almost by chance, it seemed, I'd become a righteous, vocal Asian American. All it had taken was a stage and a villain.

That's how it is with Asian American identity—nothing brings it out like other people's expectations and a sense of danger. Until recently, I rarely self-identified as "Asian American." I might say "Chinese American," if asked. Otherwise, pointedly, "American." But there are times when what you choose to call yourself becomes irrelevant. Ask Tiger Woods, whose insistence that he was "Cablinasian" didn't keep the media from blackening him, when he first arrived, into golf's Jackie Robinson. There are times when other people *need* to think of you as X, even if you believe you are Y. This was one of those times. I was in the studio to speak *as an Asian American.*

Of course, I was complicit in this casting; I chose to take the role. What was curious to me, however, is how I managed, if even for a moment, to lose myself in it. Here is where the sense of danger came into play. I may not have started out being terribly exercised about the perils of Yellow Peril stereotyping. But once I perceived the smarmy hypocrisy of this fellow—once I heard his intransigent insistence that the fault lay only with whiny, race-peddling Asians like me—I was chilled by the sense that maybe there *is* a danger out there. Maybe it *is* true, as I was then asserting on camera, that what separates insulting caricatures from more troubling forms of anti-Asian sentiment is only a slippery slope. At that moment I began to comprehend the most basic rationale for pan-Asian solidarity: self-defense.

I still understand that rationale, and many others. I understand, that is, why so many Americans of various ethnic origins have chosen, over the last generation, to adopt a one-size-fits-all "Asian American" identity. It is an affirming counterstatement to the narrative in which yellow people are either foreigners or footnotes. It is a bulwark against bigotry. It is, perhaps most important, a community. I can recount the ways, over the years, that I've become more Asian American myself. I've learned the appropriate cultural and political references. I've become familiar with the history. And of course, I've spoken out against Asian-bashing on national television.

Nevertheless, the fact remains: I am not an Asian American activist; I just play one on TV. Even though I have a grasp of why this identity matters, I cannot escape the feeling that it is contrived and, in a more profound way, unnecessary. In a way, I envy those who choose to become wholeheartedly Asian American: those who believe. At least they have a certain order to their existence. I, on the other hand, am an accidental

Asian. Someone who has stumbled onto a sense of race; who wonders now what to do with it.

4.

We are inventors, all. We assemble our selves from fragments of story.

Every identity is a social construction, a drawing of arbitrary lines. But are all identities *equally* arbitrary—and equally necessary? It's worthwhile to compare a racial identity like "Asian American" with what might be said to exist "within" it (ethnicity) and "around" it (nation).

An ethnic identity like "Chinese" matters because it is a medium of cultural continuity and meaning. "Chineseness," to be sure, is not an easy thing to delineate. It is a simplified marker for a complex reality. But the fact is that when I speak of my heritage—or when I speak of losing my heritage—I am referring to sounds and stories and customs that are *Chinese* American.

National identity, in the American case, is more problematic. It is far-flung and often contradictory. It is more reliant on myth and paradox than many other national identities. It is not, however, empty of meaning. America matters in both a civic sense and a cultural one. As a state, it is a guarantor of unmatched freedoms. As a place, it is an unrivaled incubator of ambition. The syntheses that America generates are, for better and worse, what pushes humanity forward today.

Race matters, too, of course. The difference is, race matters mainly because race matters. It's undeniable, in other words, that society is still ordered by the random bundle of traits we call "race"—and that benefits and penalties are often assigned accordingly. But it is this persistent social fact, more than any *intrinsic* worth, that makes racial identity deserving of our moral attention.

Don't get me wrong: it's not that I wish for a society without race. At bottom, I consider myself an identity libertarian. I wish for a society that treats race as an option, the way white people today are able to enjoy ethnicity as an option. As something cost-free, neutral, fluid. And yet I know that the tendency of race is usually to solidify: into clubs, into shields.

To a great degree, then, my misgivings about racial identity flow from a fear of ethnosclerosis: the hardening of the walls between the races. But perhaps my worries, like the pageants of difference that prompted them, belong to a time that is already passing. Perhaps over the horizon, beyond multiculturalism, awaits the cosmopolitan realm that David Hollinger calls "postethnic America." And perhaps there is no way to call forth this horizon but with the stories we have at hand.

5.

I have a friend from college who used to be a deracinated East Coast suburban ABC—someone, in other words, quite like me. When he moved to the West Coast for graduate school, though, he got religion. He was, for the first time, in a place where Asian Americans were not few and far between. He joined the Asian student union, began reading Asian American journals and literature anthologies, spent more and more of his days with Asian friends, entered into his first relationship with a girl who wasn't white (she was Japanese, to the vexation of his parents). Soon he was speaking to me in earnest about the importance of being Asian. And he seemed genuinely happy, at ease.

It's not hard to see why my friend became what I call a "born-again Asian." He had found fellowship and, with the fellowship, meaning. He had found a place where he would always fit in, always be recognized. He had found a way to fill a hole, the gnawing sense of heritage deficit that plagues many a second-generation banana. And the mortar he was using was not anything so ancient and musty as Chinese civilization; it was a new, synthetic, made-in-the-U.S.A. adhesive called "Asianness." For my friend, this was *exciting* as well as fulfilling.

My own conversion, if I can call it that, is far from complete. Having spent so much of my life up through college soft-pedaling my Asianness, I began afterward to realize how unnecessary that had been. I began, tentatively, to peel back the topmost layers of my anti-race defenses. Did I have an epiphany? No; I think I simply started to grow up. I became old enough to shed the mask of perpetual racelessness; old enough, as well, to sense in myself a yearning for affinity, for *affiliation*. So I joined a couple of Asian American organizations, began going to their meetings and conventions. And I was welcome. Nobody questioned my authenticity, my standing. Mainly I encountered people quite like me: second-generation, mainstream, in search of something else. Soon I was conversant in the patois of "the community." Soon I was calling myself, without hesitation, "Asian American."

Don't give me too much credit, though. The truth is, I was mainly exploring the public, institutional, side of Asian America. The private side, the realm of close friendships formed through race, I have entered only lately. Perhaps the most you could say of me is that I am an assimilist in recovery: once in denial, now halfway up the twelve-step to full, self-actualized Asian Americanness. I am glad to have climbed this far and to have left behind some insecurities. I am not sure, however, how much farther I should go.

6.

Thirty-some years ago, there were no "Asian Americans." Not a single one. There were Japanese Americans, Chinese Americans, Filipino Americans, and so on: a disparate lot who shared only yellow-to-brown skin tones and the experience of bigotry that their pigmentation provoked. Though known to their countrymen, collectively, as "Orientals," and assumed to share common traits and cultures, they didn't think of themselves at all as a collective. It really wasn't until the upheavals of the late 1960s that some of them began to.

Stirred by the precedent of Black Power, a cadre of Asian student activists, mostly in California, performed an act of conceptual jujitsu: they would create a positive identity out of the unhappy fact that whites tend to lump all Asians together. Their first move was to throw off the "Oriental" label, which, to their thinking, was the cliché-ridden product of a colonial European gaze. They replaced it with "Yellow," and after protests from their darker-hued constituents, they replaced "Yellow" with "Asian American." In their campaign for semantic legitimacy, the ex-Orientals got an unlikely assist from bean-counting federal bureaucrats. Looking to make affirmative action programs easier to document, the Office of Management and Budget in 1973 christened the term *Asian and Pacific Islander* for use in government forms. In the eyes of the feds, all Asians now looked alike. But this was a *good* thing.

The greatest problem for "Asian America," at least initially, was that this place existed mostly in the arid realm of census figures. It was a statistical category more than a social reality. In the last few decades, though, Asian American activists, intellectuals, artists, and students have worked, with increasing success, to transform their label into a lifestyle and to create, by every means available, a truly pan-ethnic identity for their ten million members. They have begun to build a nation.

The scholar Benedict Anderson has aptly defined the nation as an "imagined community," a grouping that relies for cohesion on an intangible, exclusive sense of connection among its far-flung members. Sometimes a nation has a state to enforce its will, sometimes it does not. But it must *always* have a mythology, a quasi-official culture that is communicated to all who belong, wherever they may be.

The Asian American narrative is rooted deeply in threat. That is one of the main things polyglot Americans of Asian descent have had in common: the fear of being discriminated against simply on account of being, metaphorically if not genetically, Chinamen. It is no accident that an early defining skirmish for Asian American activists was the push for Asian American Studies programs at San Francisco State and Berkeley in 1968. For what these programs did, in part, was to record and transmit the history of mistreatment that so many immigrants from Asia had endured over the centuries. Today, in the same vein, one of the most powerful allegories in Asian American lore is the tale of Vincent Chin, a Chinese American beaten to death in 1982 by two laid-off white auto workers who took him to be Japanese. The Chin story tells of a lingering strain of vicious, indiscriminate racism that can erupt without warning.

Yet no race can live on threat alone. To sustain a racial identity, there must be more than other people's racism, more than a negation. There must also be an affirmative sensibility, an aesthetic that emerges through the fusing of arts and letters with politics. Benedict Anderson again, in *Imagined Communities*, points to vernacular "print-capitalism"—books, newspapers, pamphlets—as the driving force of an incipient national consciousness. On the contemporary scene, perhaps no periodical better epitomizes the emerging aesthetic than the New York–based bimonthly A. *Magazine: Inside Asian America.*

Founded eight years ago by a Harvard graduate and entrepreneurial dynamo named Jeff Yang, A. *Magazine* covers fashion, politics, film, books, and trends in a style one might call Multiculti Chic. To flip through the glossy pages of this publication is to be swept into a cosmopolitan, cutting-edge world where Asians *matter.* It is to enter a realm populated by Asian and Asian American luminaries: actors like Jackie Chan and Margaret Cho, athletes like Michael Chang and Kristi Yamaguchi. It is to see everyday spaces and objects—sporting events, television shows, workplaces, bookstores, boutiques—through the eyes of a well-educated, socially conscious, politically aware, media-savvy, left-of-center, twenty-to-thirty-something, second-generation Asian American. It is to create, and be created by, an Ideal Asian.

There is something fantastic about all this, and I mean that in every way. That the children of Chinese and Japanese immigrants, or Korean and Japanese, or Indian and Pakistani, should so heedlessly disregard the animosities of their ancestors; that they should prove it possible to reinvent themselves as one community; that they should catalog their collective contributions to society so very sincerely: what can you say, really, but "Only in America"? There is an impressive, defiant ambition at work here: an assertion of ownership, a demand for respect. But there is also, on occasion, an under-oxygenated air of fantasy, a shimmering mirage of whitelessness and Asian self-sufficiency. A *dream.*

The dream of a nation-race called Asian America makes the most sense if you believe that the long-discredited "melting pot" was basically replaced by a "quintuple melting pot." This is the multicultural method at its core: liquefy the differences *within* racial groups, solidify those *among* them. It is a method that many self-proclaimed Asian Americans, with the most meliorative of intentions, have applied to their own lives. They have thrown the *chink* and the *jap* and the *gook* and the *flip* into the same great bubbling cauldron. Now they await the emergence of a new and superior being, the *Asian American.* They wish him into existence. And what's troubling about this, frankly, is precisely what's inspiring: that it is possible.

The invention of a race testifies not only to the power of the human imagination but also to its limits. There is something awesome about the coalescence of a sprawling conglomerate identity. There is something frustrating as well, the sense that all this creativity and energy could have been harnessed to a greater end. For the challenge today is not only to announce the arrival of color. It is also to form combinations that lie beyond color. The creators of Asian America suggest that racial nationalism is the most meaningful way of claiming American life. I worry that it defers the greater task of confronting American life.

7.

Power. Race, in the guise of whiteness, has always been about power. Now, in the masks of color, it is also about countervailing power. To call yourself a minority today is not only to acknowledge that you are seen by whites as nonwhite. It can also be to choose, as a matter of vocation, to sustain the dichotomy.

Frank Wu, a law professor and correspondent for *Asian-Week*, once wrote a candid and elegant essay in which he confessed to becoming a Professional Asian American. "Much like someone who becomes famous for being famous," he wrote, "I am making a career out of my race." He is not alone, of course, in his career choice. Over the last twenty years, there has been a proliferation of pan-Asian associations, advocacy groups, and political lobbies. These groups offer their members connections, capital, standing, protection. They do important work on behalf of those without a voice. Together, they represent the bureaucratization—the mechanization, really—of the race. The Professional Asian Americans who run these groups have learned well from their black and Hispanic counterparts that *if you build it, they will come:* if you construct the institutions that a "legitimate" race is supposed to have, then people will treat your race as legitimate.

One thing Professional Asian Americans are quick to point out is that they are not honorary whites. Fair enough: one would like to be able to do well in this country without being called white. And one should be able to address the fact that plenty of Asian Americans, unlike "real" whites, still pay a social penalty for their race. But something Professional Asian Americans sometimes overlook is that they are not honorary blacks either. African Americans created the template for minority politics in this country. That template, set in the heavy type of protest and opposition, is not always the best fit for Asian Americans. For Asian Americans haven't the moral purchase that blacks have upon our politics.

Asian Americans belong not to a race so much as to a confederation, a big yellow-and-brown tent that covers a panoply of interests. And while those interests converge usefully on some points—antidiscrimination, open immigration—they diverge on many others. This is a "community," after all, that consists of ten million people of a few dozen ethnicities, who have roots all across America and around the globe, whose families have been here anywhere from less than a week to more than a century, whose political beliefs run the ideological gamut, who are welfare mothers and multimillionaires, soldiers and doctors, believers and pagans. It would take an act of selective deafness to hear, in this cacophony, a unitary voice.

Without a unitary voice, however, there can never be maximum leverage in the bargaining for benefits. There can be no singular purpose for the Professional Asian American, no stable niche in the marketplace of identities. It will grow ever harder to speak of "the race." So be it. What will remain is the incalculable diversity of a great and growing mass of humanity. And there, in the multitudes, will lie a very different kind of power.

8.

What maketh a race?

To people in China, the Chinese constitute a single race. Except, that is, for those Chinese who aren't Chinese; those who aren't of the dominant Han group, like the Miao or Yao or Zhuang or whatever. They belong to separate races.

To the Chinese, Indians are a single, and separate, race. But "Indian," to many Indians, is like "Asian American" to me: an artificial, monochrome label. The distinctions that matter in India are between Bengalis and Punjabis and Gujeratis and others.

74

To the Japanese, who certainly think of themselves as a race, the Chinese, Indians, and Koreans are all separate races. To the Koreans, the Filipinos are; to the Filipinos, the Vietnamese. And so on.

To the Anglos who founded the United States, the Irish who arrived in great waves in the early nineteenth century were a separate race. To the Germans who killed Jews in this century and the French who watched, the Jews were a separate race. To the blacks of America, the Anglos and the Irish and the Germans and French and the Jews have always ended up being part of the same, and separate, race.

To the judiciary system of the United States, Asian Indians were held to be: probably not white (1909), white (1910), white again (1913), not white (1917), white (1919 and 1920), not white (1923), still not white (1928), probably never again white (1939 and 1942).

To those who believe in race, the spaces in between are plugged tight with impurities: quadroons, octoroons, mulattoes, morenas, mutts, mongrels, half-castes, half-breeds, halfies, hapas.

To those who do not believe, there is only this faith: the mixed shall inherit the earth.

What maketh a race is not God but man. What maketh a race is only the sin of self-love.

9.

Last May, I received in the mail a calendar of events and exhibits "celebrating Asian Pacific American Heritage Month." Here is what it included: A Celebration of APA Women's Leadership into the Twenty-first Century. An APA Spring Benefit. An APA Scholarship Dinner. An APA Performance Series. An APA Writers' Reading. A Performance of Music in the Lives of APAs. An APA Heritage Festival. (The theme this year: "One Vision, One Mission, One Voice.")

When I read the calendar the first time, I took all the information at face value, noted a few events that sounded interesting. When I read it a second time, a question pressed its way through the hazy membrane of multiculturalism in my brain and presented itself starkly, even rudely: What the heck is an "APA"?

If "Asian Pacific American" is an overbroad generalization, then what is "APA" but a soulless distillation of an overbroad generalization? I know it's a typographical and linguistic convenience, like the "USA" in USA Today. But the truncation and abbreviation of experience that the label perpetrates reflects the truncation and abbreviation of reasoning that you'll find in the call for celebration.

I agree that in the form of a coalition—that is, as a set of political alliances among organized groups—the Asian American identity can be quite important. But it is not a coalition that I am being asked to celebrate. It is a race: a discrete entity

with "one vision, one mission, one voice." A race, which is supposed to be more primordial than any temporary, tactical
alliance. A race, which apparently does not need justification
for its existence but merely *is*. One celebrates the race as a matter of tradition, because it is there. Moreover, to celebrate the
race is to nourish it, to sustain it. And that is precisely what
gives me pause.

In a provocative book called *The Rise and Fall of Gay Culture*, Daniel Harris describes the way that the longtime isola-
tion of the gay community inspired an intensely creative and
pointedly oppositional gay culture. Now that intolerance and
ostracism are declining, Harris says, elements of that subculture are being coopted by the mainstream: assimilated. He
laments this fact, because in his view, a real cultural legacy is
disappearing. But he does not lament it so much that he wishes
for a return to the kind of homophobia that had yielded the
subculture in the first place. Gay culture is no longer so necessary, Harris reluctantly acknowledges, and this is a triumph as
much as it is a tragedy.

The case of gay culture is relevant because it raises the big
questions of identity politics: After discrimination subsides, is it
still necessary for a minority group to keep the cultural wagons
circled? Should walls that once existed to keep a minority
group *out* now be maintained to keep them *in*? Should a
prison of identity be converted, upon liberation, into a home?
It seems that many who cheer Asian Pacific American Heritage Month are saying "yes" to these questions.

I don't mean to suggest that Asian Americans are able to live bigotry-free lives today, or that most Asian American activists are cultural segregationists, or that the gay community provides a perfect parallel to the Asian community. What I am saying, simply, is that more than ever before, Asian Americans are only as isolated as they want to be. They—we—do not face the levels of discrimination and hatred that *demand* an enclave mentality, particularly among the second generation, which, after all, provides most of the leadership for the nation-race. The choice to invent and sustain a pan-Asian identity is just that: a choice, not an imperative.

When you think about it, though, this choice seems almost like a reflex, a compensatory reaction to a derogatory action. What troubles me about becoming Asian American is not that it entails associating with a certain kind of person who, in some respects, is like me. What troubles me is associating with a certain kind of person whose similarity to me is defined on the primary basis of pigmentation, hair color, eye shape, and so forth. On the basis, that is, of the very badge that was once the source of stigma. This progression is natural, perhaps even necessary. But it lends a fragile quality to calls for "Asian American pride." For what is such pride, in this light, but shame turned upside down?

There are, of course, many ways to be Asian American: single-mindedly, offhandedly, out of conviction, out of convention. Racial identity needn't be an all-or-none proposition. But the more I have had occasion to let out my "inner Asian," the more I have felt a tinge of insincerity. For it is as if I were applying a salve to a wound I am not even sure I have, nursing a memory of exclusion and second-class treatment that people who look like me are presumed to suffer. Is this memory of wounds, this wounded memory, really mine? Is there anything more to my "APA-ness"?

10.

What's missing from Asian American culture is culture.

The idea seems absurd at first. No Asian American culture? What about Zen Buddhism, feng shui, karaoke bars? Well, yes. The problem, though, is that these and other forms of culture inherited by Asian Americans are *ethnic* in origin. The folkways are Chinese, for example, not "Asian." The holidays are Vietnamese, the language Korean, the dress Japanese. As far as an organically *pan-Asian* culture is concerned, there isn't much there. As one Asian American activist once said tellingly, "I think Asian American culture is anything that Asian Americans are doing. Just that."

Does the same logic apply to "Asian American history"? There is something undeniably powerful about a work like *Strangers from a Different Shore*, Ronald Takaki's synoptic history of Asian Americans. Chinese laborers built the railroads and challenged discriminatory laws, Japanese Americans fought for principle and for country in World War II. More people should know about these and other legacies. But herding such facts under the heading of "Asian American history" feels faintly like anachronism. In a subtle way, it ascribes to distinct ethnic communities of the past the pan-ethnic mind-set of the present. It serves to create collective memory *retroactively.*

Collective memory, like individual memory, can of course be constructed after the fact. But it has greater force in the world when it derives from a past of collective action and shared experience. And that is something that Asian Americans—*as* Asian Americans—have had for only two or three decades. That's why, compared with the black or Jewish or even Latino identity, the Asian American identity seems so awfully incoherent. Unlike blacks, Asians do not have a cultural idiom that arose from centuries of thinking of themselves as a race; unlike Jews, Asians haven't a unifying spiritual and historical legacy; unlike Latinos, another recently invented community, Asians don't have a linguistic basis for their continued apartness. While the Asian American identity shares with these other identities the bones of collective victimization, it does not have their flesh of cultural content.

It is more meaningful, I think, to celebrate Korean or Vietnamese or Chinese heritage—something with an identifiable cultural core. Something deeper than a mere label. Ultimately, though, my objection is not only to the APA label; it is to the labeling mind itself. The hunger for ethnic heritage is a hunger for classification, for the nostalgic certainty of place. "Heritage" offers us a usable past, coded easily by color. It does not tell us enough about how we—we of every color—should fashion a workable future.

Let me admit: When I read accounts of growing up Nisei in the middle of the century, when I read short stories by Indian immigrants about the struggle of life here, or when I read poems by the children of those immigrants, poems of loss and discovery, I feel connected to something. I find it easy to see in these characters and to hear in their diction the faces and voices of my own family. The scents, textures, and rhythms of my childhood come speeding into vibrant immediacy. This, the knowledge of cross-cultural connection, the possibility of pan-Asian empathy, is something to be valued.

But why, in the end, should empathy be skin-deep? Experiences like migration, generational conflict, language barriers, and ostracism are not the sole province of Asians or any other "race." I admire many Asian American writers who deal in such themes. I cannot get enough of Chang-Rae Lee's work. I quite enjoy Gish Jen. I find David Mura and Shawn Wong powerful. But at the same time, some of the most resonant scenes of youthful acculturation I ever read were to be found in Philip Roth's *Portnoy's Complaint*. Or *Colored People*, by Henry Louis Gates, Jr. Or Richard Rodriguez's *Hunger of Memory*. Or Norman Podhoretz's *Making It*.

I define my identity, then, in the simplest way possible: according to those with whom I identify. And I identify with whoever moves me.

11.

No identity is stable in today's wild, recombinant mix of culture, blood, and ideas. Things fall apart; they make themselves anew. Every race carries within it the seeds of its own destruction.

Today, close to 50 percent of Asian Americans under thirty-five are marrying non-Asians, which promises rather quickly to change the meaning of the race. At the same time, growing numbers are reconstituting themselves into subcommunities of ethnicity, spurred by the Indian, Filipino, Korean, and other "Asian" Americans who have at times felt like extras in this Chinese- and Japanese-dominated show. Meanwhile, mass immigration has made for an Asian American population that is now two-thirds foreign-born, and among many recent arrivals, a pan-Asian identity seems uncomfortable and unnecessary. Finally, the accelerating whirl of global capitalism now means that the most noteworthy kind of Asian American culture may be Asian/American culture: fads and fashions that arrive directly from Asia; things you don't have to be Asian American to enjoy or to claim.

To put it simply: the Asian American identity as we now know it may not last another generation. Which makes doubters like me grow more doubtful—and more hopeful. There was something about the creation of this race, after all, that embodied the spirit of the times: compensatory, reactive, consumed with what Charles Taylor calls "the politics of recognition." There is something now about the mutation of the race that reflects a change in that spirit. If whiteness was once the thesis of American life, and colored cults of origin the antithesis, what remains to be written is the synthesis. From the perspective of my children and their children, from the perspective, that is, of those who will *be* the synthesis, it may seem that "Asian American" was but a cocoon: something useful, something to outgrow. And in this way, the future of the race may reflect the future of race itself. A future beyond recognition.

12.

I am speaking now to a group of students, mostly freshmen and sophomores, at a small midwestern college. It is Asian Pacific American Heritage Month, and the students are members of the Asian Student Association. I have come to implore them to get more involved in politics, in public life.

College is supposed to be where Americans of Asian descent become Asian Americans, where the consciousness is awakened. But not this college. The students, improbably, are looking to me for guidance. Though they haven't said it in so many words, they want to know why it is they gather. They want to know what it is, besides the fact that there are so few of them on this white prairie campus, that should bring and hold them together; what, besides great potluck dinners, there is for them to *do*.

I am tempted for a moment to preach the gospel of The Individual, of the "unencumbered self" who has transcended such trivialities as race. I consider telling them that the Asian American identity is a leaky raft and that they had better learn to swim. But I don't have the heart to say any of this. For I, too, am of two minds. Instead, I tell them they should search for meaning as Asian Americans, if they so choose, or as whatever variety of self they feel free to express. So long as they feel free.

Afterward, I join a few students for dinner at a local Japanese restaurant. It is a nice place, spare and serene. We order, and then the oldest among them thanks me formally for coming to their school. For a few minutes, their attention is focused on me; they ask questions about my work, my opinions. Pretty soon, though, they're just talking to one another, in two or three different conversations, laughing, telling tales, flirting. That's all right with me. I am a stranger to them, after all, an outsider who doesn't know their stories. I am here by accident. And so I sit back, quietly, as they share their meal.

The
Chinatown
Idea

There is a map. In a book I am reading about Chinatown there is a map of lower Manhattan that marks off those precincts where the "proportion of Chinese" is 46 percent or more. It is tidy, this grid of black and white rectangles, a demographer's false imposition of order. And yet it is also perfectly apt. For this is how we know Chinatown, how we prefer to discover it: as a series of shaded cantons, discrete and contained. This map will never attest to the flesh and mortar of the streets; it cannot tell the history of those ancient tenements where the Fuzhounese are sedimented atop the Cantonese atop the Puerto Ricans atop the blacks atop the Jews. It reveals nothing about the ragged topography of private lives. But what it does chart with sad precision is the mentality, the love of clean boundary, that makes Chinatown so sadly sovereign. It is, in the end, a map of our own partitioned soul.

In suburbs like the one I grew up in, Chinese restaurants marooned in strip malls took great pains to advertise their "authentic Chinese cuisine." In the streets of Chinatown, of course, such claims are unnecessary, as redundant as they would be in China itself. Chinatown is *presumed* authentic: the food, the people, the way of life. This is what real Chinese-ness is supposed to be.

When I was a boy, my family went on a day trip to the "Amish country" of Lancaster County, Pennsylvania. I remember the trip vividly. I was wearing a green-and-yellow-striped shirt, blue shorts, new Pumas, a Yankees cap. I recall the dusty farm road we drove down, the black hats and vests of the Amish, the smell of the barnyard everywhere, the crunching rickety passage of horse-drawn wagons. What I remember most, however, is meeting the eyes of an Amish boy about my age. He stared back at me, pale and expressionless, as if from a history book. To me, this was a boy already dead, consigned to live out his days in someone else's past. And I, I must have seemed to him equally improbable: the face of a strange future, one that hadn't quite arrived but had already passed him by.

The encounter left an impression on me. As we were leaving, I asked my father to buy me a doll at the gift shop, a plastic Amish boy in full costume. I brought the doll home and laid him snugly in his box.

We all like to have our Amish, I suppose: living exhibits of prelapsarian purity; monuments to our pilgrim's progress; sad, ceremonial totems of an assimilation beyond repair. But somewhere deep down, we suspect that the objects of our gaze have eyes of their own. That in the indecipherable script of their lives is more meaning than we may know.

———

For more than two decades, my mother's mother, Po-Po, lived in a cinder-block one-bedroom apartment on the edge of New York's Chinatown. She was twenty floors up, so if you looked straight out from the main room, which faced north, one block appeared to melt into the next, all the way to the spire of the Empire State off in the distance. This was a saving grace, the view, since her own block down below was not much to look at. Her building, one of those interchangeable towers of 1970s public housing, was on the lower east side of the Lower East Side, at the corner of South and Clinton. It was, as the realtors say, only minutes from the Brooklyn Bridge and South Street Seaport, although those landmarks, for all she cared, might as well have been in Nebraska. They weren't part of the world Po-Po inhabited, which was the world that I visited every few months during the last years of her life.

My visits followed a certain pattern. I'd get to her apartment around noon, and when I knocked on the door I could hear her scurrying with excitement. When she opened the door, I'd be struck, always as if for the first time, by how tiny she was: four feet nine and shrinking. She wore loose, baggy clothes, nylon, and ill-fitting old glasses that covered her soft, wrinkled face. It was a face I recognized from my own second-grade class photo. *Eh, Po-Po, ni hao maaa?* She offered a giggle as I bent to embrace her. With an impish smile, she proclaimed my American name in her Yoda-like voice: *Areek.* She got a kick out of that. As she shuffled to the kitchen, where Li Tai Tai, her caregiver, was preparing lunch, I would head to the bathroom, trained to wash my hands upon entering Po-Po's home.

In the small bath were the accessories of her everyday life: a frayed toothbrush in a plastic Star Trek mug I'd given her in 1979, stiff washrags and aged pantyhose hanging from a clothesline, medicine bottles and hair dye cluttered on the sinktop. I often paused for a moment there, looking for my reflection in the filmy, clouded mirror, taking a deep breath or two. Then I would walk back into the main room. The place was neat but basically grimy. Some of the furniture—the lumpy couch, the coffee table with old magazines and congealed candies, the lawn chair where she read her Chinese newspaper through a magnifying glass—had been there as long as I could remember. The windowsill was crammed with plants and flowers. The only thing on the thickly painted white wall was a calendar. *Your house looks so nice,* I'd say in a tender tone of Mandarin that I used only with her. On a tray beside me, also surveying the scene, was a faded black-and-white portrait of Po-Po as a beautiful young woman dressed in Chinese costume. *Lai chi ba,* Po-Po would say, inviting me to eat.

Invariably, there was a banquet's worth of food awaiting me on the small kitchen table: *hongshao* stewed beef, a broiled fish with scallions and ginger, a leafy green called *jielan,* a soup with chicken and winter melon and radishes, tofu with ground pork, stir-fried shrimp still in their salty shells. Po-Po ate sparingly, and Li Tai Tai, in her mannerly Chinese way, adamantly refused to dine with us, so it was up to me to attack this meal. I gorged myself, loosening my belt within the half hour and sitting back dazed and short of breath by the end. No matter how much I put down, Po-Po would express disappointment at my meager appetite.

As I ate she chattered excitedly, pouring forth a torrent of opinions about politics in China, Hong Kong pop singers, the latest developments in Taiwan. After a while, she'd move into stories about people I'd never met, distant relations, half brothers killed by the Communists, my grandfather, who had died when I was a toddler. Then she'd talk about her friends who lived down the "F" train in Flushing or on the other side of Chinatown and who were dying one by one, and she'd tell me about seeing Jesus after she'd had a cancer operation in 1988, and how this blond Jesus had materialized and said to her in Chinese, *You are a good person, too good to die now. Nobody knows how good you are. Nobody appreciates you as much as I do.* I would sit quietly then, not sure whether to smile. But just as she approached the brink she would take a sip of 7UP and swerve back to something in the news, perhaps something about her heroine, the Burmese dissident Aung San Suu Kyi. She was an incredible talker, Po-Po, using her hands and her eyes like a performer. She built up a tidal momentum, relentless, imaginative, spiteful, like a child.

I generally didn't have much to say in response to Po-Po's commentary, save the occasional Chinese-inflected *Oh?* and *Wah!* I took in the lilt of her Sichuan accent and relied on context to figure out what she was saying. In fact, it wasn't till I brought my girlfriend to meet Po-Po that I realized just how vague my comprehension was. *What did she say?* Carroll would ask. *Um, something about, something, I think, about the president of Taiwan.* Of course, I'm not sure Po-Po even cared whether I understood. If I interjected, she'd cut me off with a hasty *bushide—no, it's not that*—a habit I found endearing in small doses but that my mother, over a lifetime, had found maddening.

If there was a lull, I might ask Po-Po about her health, which would prompt her to spring up from her chair and, bracing herself on the counter, kick her leg up in the air. *I do this ten times every morning at five,* she would proudly say in Chinese. *Then this,* she'd add, and she would stretch her arms out like little wings, making circles with her fingertips. *And last week I had a headache, so I rubbed each eye like this thirty-six times.* Pretty soon I was out of my chair, too, laughing, rubbing, kicking, as Po-Po schooled me in her system of exercises and home remedies. We did this every visit, like a ritual.

Time moved so slowly when I was at Po-Po's. After lunch, we might sit on the couch next to each other or go to her room so she could tell me things that she didn't want Li Tai Tai to hear. We would rest there, digesting, our conversation turning more mellow. I might pull out of my bag a small keepsake for her, a picture of Carroll and me, or a souvenir from a recent vacation. She would show me a bundle of poems she had written in classical Chinese, scribbled on the backs of the small cardboard rectangles that come with travel packs of Kleenex. She would recount how she'd been inspired to write this poem or that one. Then she would open a spiral notebook that she kept, stuffed with news clippings and filled with idioms and sentences she had copied out of the Chinese newspaper's daily English lesson: *Let's get a move on. I don't like the looks of this.* At my urging, she'd read the sentences aloud, tentatively. I would praise her warmly, she would chuckle, and then she might show me something else, a photo album, a book about *qigong.*

One day she revealed to me her own way of prayer, demonstrating how she sat on the side of her bed at night and clasped her hands, bowing as if before Buddha, repeating in fragile English, *God bless me? God bless me? God bless me?* Another time she urgently recited to me a short story that had moved her to tears, but I understood hardly a word of it. On another visit she fell asleep beside me, her glasses still on, her chin tucked into itself. And so the hours would pass, until it was time for me to go—until, that is, I had decided it was time to go, for she would have wanted me to stay forever—and I would hold her close and stroke her knotted back and tell her that I loved her and that I would miss her, and Po-Po, too modest to declare her heart so openly, would nod and press a little red envelope of money into my hand and say to me quietly in Chinese, *How I wish I had wings so I could come see you where you live.*

———

Chinatown, the guidebooks will tell you, is above all an *experience:* "an assault on the senses," as Fodor's puts it. Firecrackers sputtering like cheap ammunition. The buzz of an alien tongue on every corner. Red-and-gold lanterns, swinging, wild neon lettering. Gangsters in black sedans. Roast birds hanging by their necks behind grimy windows. The waft of vented grease and burnt incense and garbage. The sound of the cook hacking up phlegm as he stir-fries your order. The bent clanging of cymbals, the beating of drums. The undulations, wild and alive, of a great festival dragon.

Sometimes I wonder: Who are those people under the dragon? Whose feet, whose legs, make that monster dance with such fury? And what face have they besides the face of this mythical beast?

———

Of all the English maxims that Po-Po picked up along the way, her favorite was probably this: "East, West, home is best." Whether she said it in earnest or with irony, I do not know.

Min-yu Tu was born in Chengdu, in Sichuan Province, in 1914. She left Chengdu for good when she ran off to get married, a coquettish student in love with her pensive, idealistic professor. He taught European history, was pained by the hypocrisy and corruption of old China. They were a modern, Western-minded couple. China was in tumult during these years, wracked by war and invasion and political intrigue. And so they moved: to Nanjing, to Chongqing, to Xian, to Lanzhou, to Taipei. When my grandfather died, Po-Po stayed in Taipei for a time. Then she decided she wanted to start over, to find fortune in America. Extravagant, impulsive was Po-Po. And so she moved, wearing a floor-length gown for her flight over the Pacific. She came to live with us, with the family of her only child, on a quiet street in Poughkeepsie. But she hadn't thought it through. She spoke no English. She knew nobody in upstate New York. She had no way to make a life for herself.

And so she moved. She had a friend, another of her husband's former students, who now worked in the New York City government. He pulled strings, got her to the top of the list for a unit in a brand-new public housing project in Chinatown. Po-Po didn't speak Cantonese. She wasn't familiar with New

York or Chinatown. But at least there she could be independent, in a place whose basic idiom she understood.

She lived in Chinatown for the rest of her life. Twenty years. She managed to make friends. She learned her way around. She joined a church, where the congregation doted on old "Tu Tai Tai." She accumulated a favorite restaurant, a favorite doctor, a favorite newsstand, a favorite market, a favorite clothing store. All the requisites of home. But did she stay in Chinatown because it had meaning, or did it have meaning only because she stayed there? To the very end, I had the sense she wanted to be somewhere else.

When Po-Po first moved to Chinatown, my mother tells me, she was full of entrepreneurial schemes: selling homemade foods, investing her mah-jongg winnings. She had dreams of grandeur. Over time, though, the dreams faded. She lacked the wherewithal, the will to make them materialize. She was in her sixties, a migrant many times over. For a while, to keep herself busy, she took a job cutting threads in a garment factory. I learned that only recently. It astonished me, because I had never thought of Po-Po as a member of the workforce; as someone with any ambition, let alone unfulfilled ambition. In a study of Chinatown's sweatshops, I read that thread-cutting is a task allowed to "lonely old ladies."

At a certain point Po-Po stopped working. She settled into a routine of seeing friends, reading the paper, shopping for necessities. She rarely left Chinatown. She must have realized then that America was to give her not a second life but only a full circling of the life she already had. East, West, East: ever in motion, ever in exile. What I never asked my grandmother was where her restless heart was home.

———

In the popular imagination, Chinatown is not so much a place as it is a metaphor—an ideograph—for all the exotic mystery of the Orient. We don't simply visit Chinatown; we *believe* in it, as surely as we believe in the ghetto or the suburb. We imbue its every peculiarity with meaning and moral import.

The Chinatown Idea holds that the people who live there should not deviate one stroke from the ways of "old China." Unless we tell them to. Consider the controversy in San Francisco about "fresh kill"—the way Chinatown butchers keep live animals around (chickens, turtles, rabbits, what-have-you) in order to ensure the freshness of their product. The reportage in the local papers can be comically ambivalent: disapproving, for this practice is said to be a threat to public health and a trespass upon the rights of animals; yet titillated, even awed, for this is exactly the sort of thing that makes Chinatown so foreign, so deliciously diverse. *What a shame it will be when this ancient Chinese folkway disappears—but disappear it must! The modern versus the traditional—an inevitable, tragic collision! In the meantime, let's take one more look at these people and their strange customs. . . .*

———

The Chinatown Idea holds too that the people who live there are not only inscrutable but indifferent. Chinatown is simply there, uninterested in the world, an island of eternity in a sea of modernity. It seems at once inert and kinetic, which is why it is such a popular cinematic backdrop: an elaborate *mise-en-scène*, rich with atmosphere and colorful props. The humans among those props—old ladies, children, whatever—are not so much alive as animated: cartoonish, they move about and chatter, but aren't supposed to have stories of their own. They exist mainly so that American characters may move past them, through them, around them.

The Chinatown Idea tells us, finally, that Chinatown *chooses* to exempt itself from America: that it is purely the product of Chinese clannishness and insularity. This is perhaps the cruelest myth. For Chinatown is nothing if not thoroughly ours. And the insularity that sustains it is not only Chinese.

———

They came to scratch gold out of the California hills, just like the Forty-niners, or to lay track across the Sierra Nevada. They usually came alone, without their wives or families. They clustered together in whatever cities they found themselves in. But they were confined to their enclaves—by law, by custom, by riot. Sometimes they were chased out altogether, as in Seattle in 1886, herded like cargo onto steamships. They were not men, in the eyes of whites, but Chinamen: beyond the pale. Excluded from the labor market, they carved out what barren niches they could. Hand laundries, restaurants. They were denied citizenship, subjected to taxes on their pigtails and to other laws. For self-protection they organized by the lines of kinship and village that had ordered their existence in China. But such was the turning of racism's screw that their tongs and associations and secret societies only confirmed white suspicions that the Chinese were an alien legion. The Chinese response to quarantine served only to perpetuate it. Thus did Chinatowns congeal in San Francisco, New York, Seattle, Boston, and other cities in the last century.

When the immigration of Chinese laborers was banned outright in 1882—as it would remain, indeed, until 1943—a generation of outcast Chinamen faced a bleak choice: return home empty-handed or remain here, condemned to life in a bachelor colony. Half remained, too poor to go back, subsisting on the vaporous hope of redemptive riches, and only gradually reckoning themselves to their fate. They whiled away the days telling stories, gambling, dreaming. By the turn of the century there were 110 males for every female in New York's Chinatown. By the eve of World War II it had become a moribund depository of men and dreams long forgotten.

That was the old Chinatown, and perhaps it would have passed into dust and dirt, like the other ethnic enclaves of America's urban past. (Unlike the Irish or Jewish enclaves,

Chinatown would have died from blockade rather than assimilation.) After the war, though, and particularly once immigration reforms in 1965 ended the quota system that had favored Europeans, new blood began to flow into the neighborhood: more women and children from China, ABC doctors and lawyers and salesmen, reform-minded Asian American activists, Hong Kong millionaires looking to park their capital, unskilled migrants desperate for work. The result, in recent decades, has been a great resurgence in New York's Chinatown.

The "new Chinatown" is a vibrant and bustling place, a sprawling bounty of curio shops, restaurants, bookstores, produce markets. Its economy and population are swelling, its borders surging outward. It has become a prime spot for sightseers, but more than that, a living community spanning the generations. New dialects and styles abound, as Fuzhounese newcomers crowd the Cantonese "natives," as cliques of Chinese American teens define and redefine what hairstyles, what poses, what clothes are cool. Always there are children going off to college, families to the suburbs or at least to Brooklyn. Chinatown is in perpetual flux, regenerating.

And yet there is still the heavy pall of the past upon this place, not merely in the aging brownstones that sag over Canal and Mott and Catherine Streets, but in the attitudes that keep those buildings packed, to the last square foot, with Chinese.

In some respects Chinatown today is as far removed from public life, as confined to the unlit realm of secrets, as it was in the last century. Certainly it has benefited from the influx of immigrants. But most of these immigrants lack the skills—particularly, the English skills—to make it beyond Chinatown. They remain in what is basically a closed economy, where Chinese employ and often exploit Chinese, where English is never spoken, and where the America of their hazy televised dreams seems a distant mirage. They become trapped. This is especially so for the untold thousands of illegal immigrants who have come in recent years. As Peter Kwong reports in his book *Forbidden Workers*, the illegals are smuggled in through an elaborate international network and enter a subterranean system of indentured servitude so vile and oppressive that it would not be tolerated anywhere in America but Chinatown.

But, alas, that is precisely the problem. The new Chinatown, like the old, is apparently not *in* America. It is a no-man's-land, where fealty to the law matters less than obeisance to "Chinese ways." In the jaundiced eye of the state, Chinatown is a zone of "home rule," where the natives govern themselves. Subminimum wages, children in sweatshops? Technicalities: the Chinese have a different standard for hard work. Blacklisting and extortion? It is not for us to judge how the Chinese do business. Occasionally, a disaster like the 1993 grounding of the *Golden Venture*, the ship carrying Chinese wage-slaves to New York, will provoke the media-political machinery to express outrage and call for corrective action. But for the most part we let the Chinese in Chinatown "take care" of one another in time-honored fashion.

They are not men, after all, but Chinamen. They have their own notions of rights and recourse. They have their peculiar methods, traditions that have accrued over a century and a half. And so we don't ask questions. We don't ask who lives behind, or beneath, the storefronts we walk past. What matters is simply that we get our cheap eats, our cheap garments. Our cheap sense of open-mindedness. This is the bargain at the heart of Chinatown.

———

Another family outing, one of our occasional excursions to the city. It was a Saturday. I was twelve. I remember only vaguely what we did during the day — Fifth Avenue, perhaps, the museums, Central Park, Carnegie Hall. But I recall with precision going to Chinatown as night fell.

We parked on a side street, a dim, winding way cluttered with Chinese placards and congested with slumbering Buicks and Chevys. The license plates — NEW YORK, EMPIRE STATE — seemed incongruous here, foreign. We walked a few blocks to East Broadway. Soon we were wading through thick crowds on the sidewalk, passing through belts of aroma: sweat and breath, old perfume, spareribs. It was late autumn and chilly enough to numb my cheeks, but the bustle all around gave the place an electric warmth. Though it was evening, the scene was lit like a stage, thanks to the aluminum lamps hanging from every produce stand. Peddlers lined the street, selling steamed buns and chicken feet and imitation Gucci bags. Some shoppers moved along slowly. Others stopped at each stall, inspecting the greens, negotiating the price of fish, talking loudly. I strained to make sense of the chopped-off twangs of Cantonese coming from every direction, but there were more tones than I knew: my ear was inadequate; nothing was intelligible.

This was the first time I had been in Chinatown after dark. Mom held Andrea's hand as we walked and asked me to stay close. People bumped us, brushed past, as if we were invisible. I felt on guard, alert. I craned my neck as we walked past a kiosk carrying a Chinese edition of *Playboy*. I glanced sidelong at the teenage ruffians on the corner. They affected an air of menace with their smokes and leather jackets, but their feathery almost-mustaches and overpermed hair made them look a bit ridiculous. Nevertheless, I kept my distance. I kept an eye on the sidewalk, too, so that I wouldn't soil my shoes in the streams of putrid water that trickled down from the alleyways and into the parapet of trash bags piled up on the curb.

I remember going into two stores that night. One was the Far Eastern Bookstore. It was on the second floor of an old building. As we entered, the sounds of the street fell away. The room was spare and fluorescent. It looked like an earnest community library, crowded with rows of chest-high shelves. In the narrow aisles between shelves, patrons sat cross-legged on the floor, reading intently. If they spoke at all it was in a murmur. Mom and Dad each found an absorbing book. They read standing up. My sister and I, meanwhile, wandered restlessly through the stacks, scanning the spines for stray English words or Chinese phrases we might recognize. I ended up in children's books and leafed through an illustrated story about the three tigers. I couldn't read it. Before long, I was tugging on Dad's coat to take us somewhere else.

The other shop, a market called Golden Gate, I liked much more. It was noisy. The shoppers swarmed about in a frenzy. On the ground level was an emporium of Chinese nonperishables: dried mushrooms, spiced beef, seaweed, shredded pork. Open crates of hoisin sauce and sesame chili paste. Sweets, like milky White Rabbit chews, coconut candies, rolls of sour "haw flakes." Bags of Chinese peanuts, watermelon seeds. Down a narrow flight of stairs was a storehouse of rice cookers, ivory chopsticks, crockery, woks that hung from the wall. My mother carefully picked out a set of rice bowls and serving platters. I followed her to the long checkout line, carrying a basket full of groceries we wouldn't find in Poughkeepsie. I watched with wonder as the cashier tallied up totals with an abacus.

We had come to this store, and to Chinatown itself, to replenish our supply of things Chinese: food and wares, and something else as well. We had ventured here from the colorless outer suburbs to touch the source, to dip into a pool of undiluted Chineseness. It was easier for my parents, of course, since they could decode the signs and communicate. But even

I, whose bond to his ancestral culture had frayed down to the inner cord of *appetite*—even I could feel somehow fortified by a trip to Chinatown.

Yet we knew that we couldn't stay long—and that we didn't really want to. We were Chinese, but we were still outsiders. When any peddler addressed us in Cantonese, that became obvious enough. They seemed so familiar and so different, these Chinatown Chinese. Like a reflection distorted just so. Their faces were another brand of Chinese, rougher-hewn. I was fascinated by them. I liked being connected to them. But was it because of what we shared—or what we did not? I began that night to distinguish between my world and theirs.

It was that night, too, as we were making our way down East Broadway, that out of the blur of Chinese faces emerged one that we knew. It was Po-Po's face. We saw her just an instant before she saw us. There was surprise in her eyes, then hurt, when she peered up from her parka. Everyone hugged and smiled, but this was embarrassing. Mom began to explain: we'd been uptown, had come to Chinatown on a whim, hadn't wanted to barge in on her unannounced. Po-Po nodded. We made some small talk. But the realization that her daily routine was our tourist's jaunt, that there was more than just a hundred miles between us, consumed the backs of our minds like a flame to paper. We lingered for a minute, standing still as the human current flowed past, and then we went our separate ways.

Afterward, during the endless drive home, we didn't talk about bumping into Po-Po. We didn't talk about much of anything. I looked intently through the window as we drove out of Chinatown and sped up the FDR Drive, then over the bridge. Manhattan turned into the Bronx, the Bronx into Yonkers, and the seams of the parkway clicked along in soothing intervals as we cruised northward to Dutchess County. I slipped into a deep, open-mouthed slumber, not awakening until we were back in Merrywood, our development, our own safe enclave. I remember the comforting sensation of being home: the sky was clear and starry, the lawn a moon-bathed carpet. We pulled into our smooth blacktop driveway. Silence. It was late, perhaps later than I'd ever stayed up. Still, before I went to bed, I made myself take a shower.

———

Strolling across the parking-lot expanse of Tiananmen Square, I see other tourists: Chinese men, from the outer provinces. From the south. They have hair and clothes as if they just rolled out of bed, or off a train. Which they probably did. They are dusty. They look at me with my Canon autofocus, or at the uniformed soldiers near Mao's tomb, or at the young women in skirts on their way to work, all with the same unyielding puzzlement.

We define by precedent. The first time I went to Hong Kong, I understood it as Chinatown minus New York plus Las

Vegas. What reference points do these rustics have for all that they now encounter? What precedent, I wonder, explains me?

I tell myself that I recognize their eyes: they are from Chinatown. Eyes that speak of bending to the world, not bending it. Eyes weathered by a knowledge of limits. Existential, unburdened by false hopes, content with the smallness of things. Then a thought occurs to me: perhaps these men are not tourists at all but drifters, migrants, desperate dreamers. I look more closely. Now I am not sure what their eyes say.

Once, in Beijing, an earnest Jimmy Carter implored Deng Xiaoping to stop restricting emigration from China to the West. Deng asked: "How many Chinese would you like?"

As China has privatized its bloated state industries, as capitalism has caught fire in the southeastern crescent of the country, dozens of millions of Chinese have been cut loose from their moorings. This so-called floating population—peasants and workers in search of riches, with little to offer but endurance—squats now on the outer rings of China's major cities. It crowds the train and bus stations to bursting. And it finds its way, by any means possible, to America. What China displaces, Chinatown embraces.

———

When I visited Chengdu, Po-Po's hometown, I used up several rolls of film. As I focused my lens on the sea of bicycles and the blood-spattered meat market, it all seemed so perfect: the good grandson retrieving a lost China for the grandmother in exile. China had changed, of course. The debris of many revolutions had piled up. But surely, I thought, she'd recognize something—a hill, a bend, a rooftop. When I showed her the pictures a few months later, she yawned. "I don't know this place," she said.

————

One representation: Chinatown is a thriving, self-sufficient community. It is a new model for Americanization, a way to make it here without falling into the decadence of the dominant culture. It is a new model for ethnic achievement, an "enclave economy" fueled by Chinese entrepreneurs and workers. It is a new model for sovereignty, swollen by the flow of capital and people from the global Chinese diaspora.

Another representation: Chinatown is a nasty, brutish shadow world. It is a Potemkin village propped up for visitors by the toil of an unseen multitude. It is a machinery of exploitation, by which power is subcontracted to front men who keep the garment factories humming, the kitchens crackling, the tenements stifling. It is a false monument to "Chinese values" like hard work and solidarity.

Which is the real Chinatown? It is a question that sociologists debate sharply. Min Zhou, in *Chinatown: The Socioeconomic Potential of an Urban Enclave*, paints roughly the first picture. Peter Kwong, in *The New Chinatown* and *Forbidden*

Workers, roughly the second. Both have lived or worked in New York's Chinatown; both are serious scholars. But neither, of course, has a monopoly on the truth.

The difficulty is not that the truth lies somewhere in between. It is that the truth lies *everywhere* in between. There are more Chinatowns than we can identify. Gangster Chinatown, Dim Sum Chinatown, Bootstraps Chinatown, Welfare Chinatown, Hipster Chinatown, Oldster Chinatown, Bay Bridge Chinatown, Manhattan Chinatown, Flushing Chinatown, Chinese Chinatown, pan-Asian Chinatown, Chinatown the ghetto, Chinatown the gateway. There are now suburban Chinatowns, like Monterey Park outside Los Angeles, places built of free choice, not necessity. There is a Chinatown for every perspective.

Personally, I find Kwong's depiction more compelling. It is gritty, stripped of illusion. There is something about Zhou's study, for all its social science jargon, that smacks of boosterism: it recalls the insincere appeals that Chinatown's business elite will sometimes issue to encourage loyalty among their laborers. *We Chinese are one great family! We take care of each other!* It sounds somewhat hollow.

But then, what authority do I really have? I, the visitor who drops in for the day? I have no experience in sweatshops, or the one-room apartments where Chinese illegals sleep packed like sardines, or the clan halls where the elders dispatch youth gangs to protect their turf. Nor do I know what pride, what comfort the dispossessed of Chinatown may take in being Chinese. All I have is a bias: a deep suspicion that the "racial loyalty" that holds Chinatown together is a pretext for something unseemly.

In the end, then, we see the Chinatown we want to see. But in the end, Chinatown sees us, too. And knows what is false about our representations.

    ————

I know a remarkable woman who works in Chinatown. Her name is Trinh Duong. She is the executive director of Chinese Staff and Workers Association, a small nonprofit that represents many of the waiters, construction workers, seamstresses, and other laborers in Chinatown. Chinese Staff, as it is called, operates out of a cramped office in the back of a dilapidated building on Catherine Street. Since its founding in 1981 Chinese Staff has been engaged in some of the more contentious economic disputes in Chinatown. To pressure restaurants and garment factories to adhere to labor laws, Chinese Staff organizes rallies, conducts media campaigns, helps workers unionize.

In 1996 the office was firebombed. Trinh mentions this almost offhandedly. She has a direct manner, a young face, a strong, low voice. She speaks with a trace of an accent, the rough edges of a 1.5-generation speaker. Not quite native.

She tells me she was born in Saigon into a merchant-class ethnic Chinese family. When she was six, her family fled Vietnam by boat. It was 1978. They spent two years in a refugee camp in Malaysia before gaining asylum in the United States. She grew up in a white town outside Reading, Pennsylvania, then attended New York University. While at NYU, she first encountered Chinatown. She was mesmerized, found the place thrilling. Never had she seen Chinese like these. She went back. One day she came across a flyer for Chinese Staff. She went to a meeting, then several more. Another Chinatown was revealed to her. She became more active. After college she quit her job at Merrill Lynch to join Chinese Staff full-time.

We are sitting at a small Cantonese restaurant now. The laminated menus are oily, the chopsticks yellowed. As she picks at the stir-fried squash, she tells me about going on a hunger strike a few years earlier. Again, so matter-of-factly that I am soon thinking to myself, Yeah, yeah, the hunger strike.

She describes her constant skirmishes with the police and the restaurant management and the factory owners and the local politicians and the other pieces of the paternalistic power structure. It sounds to me like fighting the sea, or cockroaches: the adversary is relentless, reaches every crevice. Then she recalls the day when she met a group of dim sum cart-pushers from one of the big restaurants, immigrant women her mother's age, with everything at stake, who were willing to march and picket and lie down and get arrested. That was the day Trinh realized she could, she should, commit herself to this Sisyphean work.

It occurs to me, as I listen to her, that this moment ought to be my own epiphany. That I should be inspired by her example to step out from the safety of the suburban second generation. That I can do more than simply write about injustice.

Instead, I write about writing about it.

My first impression upon meeting Trinh was that she was far more Chinese than I: engaged with the community, fluent. Also, less polished, less assimilated than I. But there are some who would consider her very un-Chinese. She speaks up, she fights, she exposes hypocrisy. She cares less about race than about basic moral courage. That, not her insider's knowledge of Chinatown, is the root of her authenticity. The irony, then, is this: I am perhaps more Americanized. She is perhaps more American.

Not long ago, I spent an afternoon in Po-Po's neighborhood. It was the first time I'd been back since she died. I wish I could tell you that I lost myself in deep reflection. But I'd gone back specifically to harvest recollections for this essay. And as I retraced the steps of our slow walks through Chinatown, I was awfully self-conscious. I must have looked like an anthropologist, scribbling impressions in my notebook.

I went into Po-Po's building, up the industrial elevator smelling of fried food, down the short hall to her door. After a pause, I rapped the metal clanger. Nobody stirred. I looked around, and noticed just how narrow the hallway was. I knocked again. Behind another door, I heard a mother yelling at her children in Spanglish. I left. When I reached the lobby an old Chinese woman was standing there, hair white and thinning.

I walked out of the lobby and onto Clinton Street. I turned left on Cherry, then cut through the yard of the La Guardia Houses, another housing project. This wasn't a bad neighborhood, I realized. Kids on swing sets, old men chatting on the benches, flowers abloom. Nobody here was white: they were Chinese, Puerto Rican, black. At the corner of Madison and Rutgers, the storefront signs began to change, from Pollo and Elegancia Nails to El Naranjo 洗衣店 (Cleaners), and from that point onward, at the East Broadway stop of the "F" train, most of the signs were in Chinese.

I wandered. I walked by the Chinese Missionary Baptist Church on Henry Street. I walked through Confucius Plaza. I walked to the Golden Unicorn restaurant, where Po-Po often took me for dim sum. I walked past the Chinese American Bank, where Po-Po put her savings account jointly in my name so that I could inherit the $1,100 or so she had saved over the years. From a distance, I looked at the Wah Wing Sang Funeral Home on Mulberry Street. I could not bring myself to go in.

Everything in Chinatown was roughly as I remembered it; whatever details I had forgotten I dutifully noted in my journal. But not until the end of my stroll, after I'd put the note-book away, did I see something truly familiar: a young woman with jet-black skin and a white blouse. I did not know her; I knew only what she was doing. She was walking at a slower gait than she was used to, and her eyes turned gently downward as her stooped-over grandmother, arm crooked in hers, inched laboriously forward.

My mother and I are peeling pears in her kitchen, crisp juicy Asian pears, one for each of us. We remember what Po-Po once told us: that it's bad luck for close relatives to *fenli*—"to split a pear"—because *fenli* can also mean "to become separated." We are talking about Mom's earliest years in America, when she lived all over New York City, working as a file clerk down-town and as a baby-sitter for room and board, saving money for college, improving her English. She was only a girl, and so free. I ask Mom whether she considered living in Chinatown when she first emigrated. "I never really thought of it," she says. I ask, because sometimes now she thinks of it.

After Po-Po died, my mother, not a planner by nature, planned everything. She searched the neighborhood for a suit-able funeral home. She traveled to Poughkeepsie to choose a plot for Po-Po in the same cemetery as my father. She spoke with the minister, called Po-Po's friends one by one.

For six days she stayed in that apartment on the edge of Chinatown. In the mornings she and Li Tai Tai emptied the closets, put things in boxes, sorted through Po-Po's hidden stashes of knickknacks and memorabilia. In the afternoons my mother walked. She walked down every alleyway and crooked street in Chinatown. She walked through Little Italy and Greenwich Village. She walked past Lincoln Center and through the Park. She walked to Morningside Heights and over to the Upper East Side. And then, as the dark of late winter descended, she walked back, mapless, guided only by memory. In the evenings she ate boiled rice at the table where Po-Po ate and she stared out the window at that view and thought of things she had never said to her mother. Finally, when everything was taken care of, she boarded a morning train to D.C., took a cab into the suburbs, and came back to the quiet enclosure of clean brick town houses where she lives.

Fear
of a
Yellow
Planet

Rising Sun

I am bathed in yellow light, my features sharpened by shadow.

I am Chinese American in a time of Chinese ascendancy. I am Chinese American: not Chinese-American, not American-Chinese, not American Chinese. I insist upon the distinction. And yet the great magnet of China, pulsating insistently, offers to pull the bottom out, to reverse my polarity. I am Chinese American at the very moment in history when the only power that truly matters in the world is Chinese or American. Which can make me valuable, in a way. And vulnerable.

There is no precedent for this, really. To be an American conjoined by blood and myth to a gigantic Asian country stirring from its slumber is to experience an odd, foreboding exhilaration. Opportunity and threat are entangled beyond distinction. China, after all, is the scene of this generation's great gold rush, the new frontier for new capitalists. (Students today are advised: Learn Chinese.) But China may also prove to be the scene of this generation's great war, or at least the source of a turbulent nonpeace. Either way, an unknown, entropic greatness looms in China, flooding forth like a swollen river, and this torrent of fortune and ambition cannot but affect me—and you. Just how, I don't yet fully know.

I know only that we are in a period of in-between today: China's status is somewhere between friend and foe; its power somewhere between impressive and alarming; its temperament between passive and aggressive. America, too, finds itself ever more in flux: between a white self-image and a colored face; between a myth of the West and a mirage of the East. For Chinese Americans, association with China hovers somewhere between romantic nostalgia and suspicious activity. But this state of in-betweenness, like the watery image in a developing photograph, cannot last forever. Things precipitate; they form.

And they form anew. What is most unsettling about China's rise, it seems, is not just that it tilts the geopolitical balance of power, but that it disturbs the idea that every race has its place. Japan once threatened to do the same thing, defying the centuries-old order that equates color with subordination, whiteness with supremacy. Then, of course, Japan lost the war. Forty years later it loomed again, until the bubble of its economy burst. Now China is the latest yellow aspirant to the superpower throne.

Whatever else happens, it is clear that the emergence of China and the opening of a "Pacific Century" will force the issue: the issue of what an American is; what an American can be. That's what is promising about the rising of this sun. But that's also what is perilous about it.

Loyalty

Do I seem scary to you? Probably not. I am a friendly-looking guy, not menacing in the least.

Do I seem foreign to you? Now, that is a more interesting question. What makes a person look foreign? There is, of course, the face. My skin is yellowish. My hair is black and straight. My eyes are brown, almond-shaped. But that is not all there is to it. Context matters, too, at least as much as content. In one memorable photograph from a trip to Beijing, I'm standing in front of the Gate of Heavenly Peace at the Forbidden City. Next to me, oblivious to the camera, is a Chinese passerby, my age roughly, my height, with something like my facial structure. There is reason to think we might be related. Yet somehow it is patently obvious who is the American in that picture. My clothes (college T-shirt, shorts, Birkenstocks), my bearing (arms akimbo), my smile (easy; straight teeth), and something else, ineffable, all give it away. My wife calls this the "Eric, but for an accident of history" picture.

Context matters. Now put my image, so obviously American, under a headline about a plot by the Chinese government to sway our elections. How do I look now? Make it a black-and-white head shot, grainy. Are you starting to wonder? Add a caption about my having "no comment." Does it occur to you suddenly that English might not be the first thing out of my mouth? Over the last year and a half I've followed with jittery interest the so-called Asian money scandal. And as I have watched the media-political complex use "shadowy" Asian American figures as a totem for fears of Chinese influence, I have heard a voice say to me more than once, "There, but for an accident of history . . ."

Not that I had anything to do with campaign fund-raising, mind you, or Asian holding companies or any such thing. (Memo to FBI: This is *not* a confession.) But I did once work in the federal government. Specifically, the part of the government that concerns itself with national security. I had the highest clearances. I worked for the Senate committee that oversees the CIA, then for the chairman of that committee, representing him on several trips abroad. Afterward I went to the State Department, and then on to the White House, where I wrote foreign policy speeches for the president. I was entrusted with some pretty heavy stuff, and no one seemed to think twice about it. But then, that was two full years before Asian people became suspect again.

One of the most recurrent rumors about my kind is that we are disloyal. Or, at best, divided in our loyalties: ever torn between an outward allegiance to this country and a hardwired fealty to some Oriental motherland. This is the suspicion that justified Chinese exclusion in 1882, and then "Asiatic" exclusion in 1924. It is a suspicion beyond ideology. Thus our enemies in World War II were, on one front, the Nazis and, on the other front, the Nips. The Germans were defined by their fascism, the Japanese by their race. At home, 110,000 innocent Japanese Americans were, *under color of law,* forced into remote detention camps for the duration of the war. As the *Los Angeles Times* memorably put it, in defense of the internment: "A viper is nonetheless a viper wherever the egg is hatched— so a Japanese-American, born of Japanese parents, grows up to be a Japanese not an American."

Surely there is nothing like that sense of menace in the air today regarding Chinese Americans or Asian Americans generally—I do not wish to overstate. But I must tell you, when the "Asian money" scandal first became a story, fed by dark mutterings in the media about subversive plots and Asian agents of influence, I got a little nervous. Was that a sneer I detected in the strained pronunciation of an unfamiliar Asian surname? Why weren't reporters distinguishing between Asian nationals and American citizens? Was it something other than simple sloth? In the period since the scandal broke, anti-Asian hate crimes have increased dramatically.

There were moments during the initial twitch of "Chinagate" hysteria when the veneer of a live-and-let-live society came peeling off a bit, exposing in many of our elites a deeply held intuition that some people are real Americans while others are just eerily American-like facsimiles. In those moments, I hastily stepped outside myself, watching for a change in people's behavior toward me, watching for a change in my own behavior. I detected none. Then I imagined what it would have been like had I still been at the White House then. Would I have been subject to greater scrutiny? Would my most innocent actions at work—speaking to my mother in Chinese on the phone, doing a bit of personal xeroxing, taking an interest in China policy—have been viewed in a more sinister light?

Sheer paranoia, I know. Oversensitivity. I've never had my loyalty questioned. No need for such anxiety. My Chinese friends and relatives are from Taiwan—they're the *good* Chinese, the anti-Communists, the ones we like. Besides, I've never actually done anything to betray my country. Never even thought about it. That should count for something, right? I'll put my worries aside, then. Keep them under wraps. Forgive me, though, if they manage occasionally to slip through.

Diaspora

Sometimes I think I will go to China to make my fortune. I am not alone in harboring this dream, of course: for a time, hardly a week went by without a reminder that China is the business opportunity of the century. But the siren song that beckons me is not just the ring of a thousand cash registers opening; it is also the call of my Chinese ancestors. *Come back*, they cry, like spirits from an Amy Tan novel. *It is your destiny.*

All right, "destiny" is a bit melodramatic—and I don't really hear those voices. Yet, as a Mandarin-speaking Chinese American, I am made to feel about not doing business in China the way Ken Griffey, Jr., might have felt had he never gone into baseball: like someone who squandered an inheritance, who failed to capitalize on a rare alignment of circumstance and skill.

I have a friend who *did* capitalize on just such an alignment. He is a few years older than me, but like me, he is an ABC who spent rather little time as a youth thinking about China or about being Chinese. He went to college, traveled the world for a time, became an investment banker in New York. Around 1991 he went to law school, but he hadn't been there more than a year when he realized that the place to be then was not in some arid classroom talking torts but in the hurly-burly of the flourishing Chinese marketplace. He quit school and joined with some friends to start a new investment bank focusing on Asian business and China-related deals. Today he is ridiculously wealthy.

It should come as no surprise that I admire this fellow terribly. But still, it is rather puzzling that I should want so badly to follow him to China. I have, after all, no particular knack for business. I have no million-dollar idea to test on a billion-plus consumers. And given Asia's financial volatility, China is no place for the clueless. That I should feel this desire testifies, I think, to the centripetal pull of Chineseness, whatever that might mean, and to the growing allure of diasporan identity.

In recent years, as the sociologist Peter Kwong has described, a cult of nationality has emerged around the so-called Overseas Chinese. These are the ethnic Chinese entrepreneurs and industrialists scattered around the globe who make the economies of Asia whir and hum. In Southeast Asia they have come to be known as the "Jews of the East," and more than any other group they have provided the capital to help fuel China's boom. China's boom, in turn, has helped fuel the myth of a great and unitary Chinese diaspora, buzzing about like bees to revitalize the mother country.

Everyone's got a reason to sustain this myth: the Chinese government, which naturally wants to encourage the inflow of investment from *huaren*; ethnic Chinese businesspeople who want to use their heritage as a calling card (or a trump card); the non-Chinese corporate executives who feel they can't "crack" this market without the *guanxi*, connections, provided by a Chinese go-between; the Western commentators and Asian politicians who want to explain China's growth in purely "civilizational" terms, as if hard work and savvy planning were Confucian in origin; the many Chinese Americans who may not benefit materially from a rich China but who collect what W. E. B. DuBois would have called the "psycho-logical wage" of knowing that China no longer seems weak or subordinate.

It's a fine myth, this vision of a borderless Chinese tribe. But it's still a myth, particularly in the American context. I, for instance, am not an Overseas Chinese. Even my mother, who reads newspapers for the Overseas Chinese, who joins Over-seas Chinese organizations and attends their meetings, is not an Overseas Chinese. She has lived here for almost forty years; she, too, has been transformed. The presumption, then, that Chinese Americans are merely Chinese people who happen to be in America, who could just as easily be in Indonesia or Malaysia, strikes me as fallacious, even dangerous. For if you insist that you belong to the diaspora, those who belong to the nation may eventually take you at your word.

I say all this in earnest. And yet if I ever had a chance to do business in China, I suspect I might change my tune. I might want to have it both ways, really: to impress my Chinese part-ners with an insider's knowledge of America, and to impress my American partners with an insider's knowledge of China. The second insider claim is much less true than the first. It is perhaps even false. Still, the possibility of profiting from such a fib helps keep the China-bound entrepreneur in me astir. What is diasporan identity, anyway, but enlightened self-interest? What is Chineseness now but another name for access? If you've got it, shouldn't you use it?

Conspiracy

The Jew has infiltrated the upper echelons of society. The Jew tries to buy the prestige he cannot naturally command. The Jew manipulates. The Jew is shrewd but not imaginative. The Jew inhabits a shadow world, wields unseen power. The Jew is not rooted in our soil. The Jew floats. The Jew has too much say in our politics. The Jew wants to run the world. The Jew covets all that you have.

If a whiff of such sentiment ever found its way into our major newspapers or into the mouths of our political leaders, you can be sure that Jewish Americans—rightly—would be apoplectic. They'd want to put a quick end to such talk. And they would be able to, in no small measure because some of them hold precisely the kind of power that all of them are rumored to hold. Only, they hold that power not so much as Jews but as *Americans.* The distinction, lost on the anti-Semite, means everything to the anti-anti-Semite.

Unfortunately, it is not yet a distinction that those with Asian surnames are granted—not, at least, to judge from the way the so-called "Asian money" scandal has played out. For everything that was said about *the Jew* in the litany above was, in the course of this scandal, said or suggested about *the Asian.* Yet the complaints were few and meek, and the prevalent view within the smart set was that those who complained were simply "playing the race card" to impede a legitimate inquest.

The scandal, in a nutshell, centered on the charge that the Chinese government funneled money through agents here— including a onetime Commerce Department official and Democratic Party fund-raiser named John Huang—to influence the outcome of the 1996 federal elections. Huang and his associates committed acts that were certainly ill-advised and quite possibly illicit. I have no brief to defend them, whether or not they were in China's employ or control. Nor do I take the allegation of a Chinese plot lightly; if true, it would be serious indeed. The problem is, there has been far more rumor than fact to this scandal, more insinuation than substantiation.

After more than a year of media scrutiny and months of grinding congressional investigation, the "Asian connection" seems more significant for what it says about Asian Americans than for what it says about our sordid campaign-finance system. For the unmistakable subtext throughout has been that Asians in America are just that—Asians in America, sojourners and foreigners.

Thus, when we first learned that Huang (a citizen) had raised over $5 million in "Asian money" for the Democrats, little differentiation was made—reportorially or morally— between contributions from abroad and contributions from Americans of Asian descent. Little effort was made to put that $5 million in the context of an $800 million campaign. Moreover, the suspicion arose that "Asian American political participation" was but a pretext for a baneful foreign agenda. And the behavior of Asian Americans was everywhere Asianized, so that the hustling of small-time players named Dean Lum or Johnny Chung was said to be typical not of American-style influence peddling but of the ancient Chinese art of using *guanxi* for self-advancement. Plying connections for access? What a devious Oriental trick!

The fact that Asian Americans could be so easily pilloried, so readily transformed into symbols of corruption, indicates how *little* power they wield, not how much. That is one of the bitter ironies of the whole affair. Another is that a ringleader of the conspiracy theorists has been William Safire, a Jew and defender of Jews. Early on, Safire fueled fears of Chinese and Chinese American treachery with snarling references to "favor-hungry foreigners," "rich aliens," "insidious networking," and "penetration by Asian interests"—just the sort of code and innuendo you'd expect from, say, *The Protocols of the Elders of Zion*.

America today has more immigrants than ever in its history. More of them than ever are coming from Asia, and more are maintaining ties to their countries of origin. More are entering our political process. And more, inevitably, will commingle domestic affairs and foreign. Could it be, then, that in this age of globalization, Americans feel the old certainties of sovereignty and identity slipping away? Could it be that Asia's resurgence will send money and people spilling over our borders? Well, yes. But surely it is possible to contemplate this without paranoid ranting. For the problem, really, is not that the Asians who come here feel divided about America; it is that America feels divided about the Asians who come here.

Citizens

Randolph Bourne, in a famous essay called "Trans-National America," argued in 1916 that American nationality should be more cosmopolitan: that we should encourage immigrants to come, to mix, to retain their ethnic attachments. Bourne wrote in a time of rising nativism, and against the parochial program of the Klan and its sympathizers. "America is coming to be," he wrote, "not a nationality but a trans-nationality, a weaving back and forth, with the other lands, of many threads of all sizes and colors." Today his voice still resonates. The America that was "coming to be" in his time has come to pass in ours.

Bourne's solution to the problem of membership in a diversifying nation was to allow for dual citizenship: loyalty to America as a matter of rights, loyalty to the old country as a matter of blood. There are intellectuals today who advocate something the same, who insist that our traditional notion of citizenship is too straitened for this era of mobile capital and fluid fidelities. Arjun Appadurai, a scholar at the University of Chicago, paints a vision of America as an ethnoracial "free-trade zone," a vast fairground for the many diasporas of the world. Others, likewise, have called for a regime of "plural patriotisms."

I share the desire to rethink American identity, particularly in the midst of today's demographic changes. And of course, I acknowledge that each of us has many varied circles of affinity. But I think calls for multiple allegiances miss the very point of American possibility. America is exceptional not only because it provides due process and a setting for free cultural expression but also because it *synthesizes* the many cultures it welcomes. Far more than in Bourne's time, America now is indeed a transnationality: an amalgamation, a seedbed for once unthinkable hybrids. It is precisely in an age of globalization that America becomes the most necessary place on earth. That is why we owe it our undivided loyalty.

Orientals

In the 1980s, when Asian Americans became the country's favorite nonwhite folk—the "model minority"—Mike Wallace of *60 Minutes* asked: "Why are Asian Americans doing so exceptionally well in school? They must be doing something right. Let's bottle it." On this view, Asian American students are something like Japanese cars: imports that imitate American forms but offer better performance, thanks to a superior Asian style of development and production. If only GM could bottle that Asian Way!

If only we could capture the genie. It's a spirit, this Asian thing. A phantasm. Just ask Deepak Chopra, whose progression from endocrinologist to mind-body healer to interpreter of wizards and spirits perfectly tracks today's gold-paved path from "Western" rationalism to "Eastern" mysticism. The Asian, apparently, is our modern-day sorcerer: the holder of powerful knowledge.

We eat up Deepak's books because they purport to tell us how to find our way—the same reason, perhaps, why so many approved of the caning of Michael Fay. Fay, you will remember, was the American teenager who in 1995 committed vandalism in Singapore and paid for it in the rear with three thwacks heard round the world. Lee Kuan Yew, Singapore's leader, took the opportunity of the caning to preach loudly about Asian rigor and American decadence. Lee, who has quite a following among the strongmen of East Asia, is an exponent of the so-called Asian Way.

The Asian Way holds that Asians, unlike non-Asians, prefer order to freedom; that Asians can suffer hardship better than non-Asians; that Asians are more disciplined and virtuous than non-Asians. All of which explains why Asians the world over seem to be doing *so exceptionally well.*

It's bad enough that people talk this way. It's worse that so many of us listen. But we do—because we Americans worry that our moral and spiritual vigor is indeed depleted. We feel lost, at millennium's end. And we believe that only the Eastern wind, only the souls of yellow folk, can guide us back.

It is an ironic twist on history, isn't it? In the age of colonialism, Europeans concocted a set of stereotypes about the weak and decadent Orient and the sensualist Eastern mentality. Orientalism, as this ideology is now known, enabled the West to feel good about "civilizing" and converting these backward natives. It also enabled the West to think of itself as "the West"—to define itself by negation. Today we have a New Orientalism, a more subtle brand—more pernicious as well, because it plays off rumors of Asian *superiority*, rather than inferiority, and because it depends on the active complicity of Asians.

The New Orientalism is the mirror image of the old. Now it is the West that is corrupted. Now it is the East that contrives to think of itself as a one-celled organism. And now, across that imagined East, it is American society that is the object of condescending fascination. But the New Orientalism is just like the old one in this regard: it depends on an artificial split of the map and the mind. It separates life cleanly into virtue and vice, East and West. And it changes nothing but the superficial order of things.

Native Son

When I was in high school, ABC kids like me were often urged by our parents to take a certain summer trip to Taiwan.

Though cloaked in the high-minded pretext of "learning your heritage," the aim of the journey, really, was to extend the Chinese bloodline. For the trip was in fact a posh cruise, known colloquially as the Love Boat, where Chinese American teenagers, under the guise of touring Taiwan, could meet, mingle, and—who knows?—perhaps one day even marry.

You have to admit, there's something refreshing about the sheer pragmatism of the parents who sent their children aboard that cruise. In America, where people are always seeking mystical bonds to an imagined past, returning to the land of one's ancestors is usually a more syrupy affair, romantic in a different sense altogether. When the motherland is in the Orient, the mystique meter is supposed to go through the roof. Certain novelists have made it a stock device to send the assimilated second-generation protagonist to China on a melodramatic search for her soul.

Well, I am assimilated, second-generation. I recently returned from China, my second trip there. And I can't help being dubious about the whole homecoming enterprise. What did I see in China? I saw a sprawling contradiction of a country beset by changes of a scale unthinkable here. I saw a nation trying to gallop into the twenty-first century while its hind legs remain in the twelfth. But while I saw many who looked like me, and many who might have been like me, I never once saw myself. That is, I never felt that transcendence the child of immigrants is supposed to experience upon going *back*. Yes, in the countryside or the ancient quarters, I could conjure up the China my grandparents knew. What never arrived, though, was the epiphany scripted for me, the sensation that I was—at last—among my own people.

Part of it was that I have no family left on the mainland. Part of it too was that I was with my redheaded wife (I never did make it to the Love Boat), and this often made us a minor spectacle, particularly in the eyes of Chinese from the outlying provinces. Mostly, I was unsure what it was I should have been searching for: Ancient fortune-tellers uttering revelatory Confucian epigrams? Long-lost relatives holding a mirror to my inner self? Mystical signs from a benevolent Chinese spirit?

These are cinematic notions of homecoming, formulaic and trite, and I scoff at them. But let me admit something: behind my sarcasm lingers a sense of disappointment. When I reflect upon it now, I feel I missed out on something during my journey to China. There is a luxury that most white Americans enjoy, and that is the luxury of ethno-banality. Roots without costs. The Sons of Italy, Daughters of Ireland, and so forth: whites can wear or remove their ancestry like a pendant. I do not feel so free. I hesitate to embrace the Old Country with full-blown sentimentality.

It shouldn't be this way, I know. During my trip I should have been able to indulge myself, to work myself into a weepy state of racial kinship. I didn't. It was my own failure of nerve, not anything anyone else said or did, that blocked me. I may have felt American as I wandered all about China. But apparently I didn't feel so American that I could pretend for a moment that I wasn't.

As it happened, the final stop in our journey was Shanghai, a glamorous, muscular city akin to what Manhattan must have been like early in this century. Of all the places I saw in China, Shanghai awakened in me the most powerful sense of affinity. Not because I had CNN in the hotel or ate Häagen-Dazs downtown, but because Shanghai, part Western and part Eastern, was something more deeply familiar: a hybrid, an amalgam, an invention, an *escape*. Standing there before the magnificent colonial buildings of the Bund, crowded now with unseen Chinese, I felt strangely at home.

Peril

Mongolphobia (n., archaic, but insidious) 1. The belief that Asians pose a threat to our way of life. 2. The fear of a yellow planet. 3. How the West was one.

The Yellow Peril. Mongol hordes. Asian invasions. It's hard to take these expressions of primal terror seriously today. They are comic-book words, lurid and sensational in the worst traditions of, well, yellow journalism. They are the stuff of proto-pulp fiction: *The Insidious Dr. Fu Manchu, the Evil Genius.*

They belong in the annals of early psychoanalysis, so obsessed are they with an unseen Other, so determinedly ignorant of Self. They seem unhinged from reality, especially from my own contemporary reality, which is not "perilous" in the least but is rather comfortable and civilized.

Yet it's not so easy to laugh this stuff off. Time and again, people in this country who considered themselves wholly civilized and rational have succumbed to exactly this sort of madness, and to devastating effect. In the late 1870s, the insecurity of white workingmen sparked wildfire riots against Chinese laborers across the West, which then gave Congress the pretext for an outright ban on Chinese immigration. In the 1940s innocent Japanese Americans were stripped of their rights because American complacency at Pearl Harbor was explained as Japanese American treachery. In the 1980s the demonization of the Japanese—and the glorification of Asian Americans as the "model minority"—was fueled by the fear that (white) America was in decline, surpassed by "those amazing Asians" who had flooded our markets and our schools. Today, America seems to be back on top, but the rise of China has some in our political class looking at Asian Americans and seeing suspicious characters.

There is progress, I suppose, in the path from lynch mobs to concentration camps to conspiracy theories. But what is galling is that in spite of generations of Asian immigration, in spite of ever-increasing contact between Asia and America,

Mongolphobia is still a ready feature of the repertoire of American avoidance mechanisms. But then, I suppose it is precisely the rise in contact that generates the anxiety we want so badly to avoid.

For much of this country's history, Asians were distant enough or few enough to serve as the perfect Manichaean scapegoats, a most necessary Evil. Asians were a monochrome screen, upon which any fear could be projected; against which heterogeneous assortments of people could magically become "white" or "American" or "Western." In the iconography of race in this century, as the historian John Dower recounts, there have generally been two states of existence for Asians: They could be subhuman (rodents, insects). They could be superhuman (monsters, machines). Either way, they were an invading force, a swarm.

Well, quietly, the invasion has in fact proceeded. In our population now there are ten million Asian Americans, which is eight million more than there were twenty-five years ago. Asian Americans have breached the mainstream; an advance guard has reached the commanding heights of power. Meanwhile, a resurgent Asia is sending wave after wave of hardy memes into our language, our manners, our dreams. Soon we may have to face a third possibility: that Asians are, in fact, human; that they have left our imaginations and arrived in our lives. Soon we may have to admit: We have already met the East, and it is us.

E.S.T.

A sampling of subject headings from *Eastern Standard Time*, a guide to Asian influence on American culture published by the editors and staff of A. *Magazine:*

Maya Lin. I. M. Pei. Porcelain. Oriental Rugs. The futon. The Kama Sutra. Hello Kitty. Speed Racer. Astro Boy. John Woo. Jackie Chan. Mighty Morphin Power Rangers. Yellow-face. Chopsticks. Chop Suey. Curry. Dim Sum. Ramen. Tea. Tofu. Woks and stir-frying. Chess. Cat's Cradle. Chutes and Ladders. Kites. Consumer electronics. Mah-jongg. Judo. Karate. Tai Chi. Origami. Nintendo. Sega. Yoga. *The Art of War.* Words: amok, avatar, bangle, bungalow, crimson, gung ho, guru, ketchup, pidgin, pundit, shampoo, thug, tycoon. Buddhism. Taoism. Feng Shui. Acupuncture. Chinese herbal medicine. Ginseng. Yo-Yo Ma. Zubin Mehta. Seiji Ozawa. Ravi Shankar. Vera Wang. Pajamas. Silk. Paisley. Indigo. Khakis. Tattoos. Asian adoptees. Nissan. Mitsubishi. Mazda. Chinatowns. The Connie Chung Syndrome (Asian female news anchors). Karaoke. Mail-order brides. Model Minority. Asian Organized Crime. Pandas.

Bridges

The first time I went to China, in 1993, I was in a delegation of congressional staff members on a "fact-finding" trip sponsored by the U.S.-Asia Institute. We were treated like VIPs. We had a guide, an interpreter, and a bus that shuttled us to meetings and to various tourist attractions. We met with high officials in key ministries. At our meals, nine-course banquets, we were given keepsake booklets embossed with our names and titles. We were definitely special, the twelve of us. But I was especially special. I was a Chinese. More, I was a Chinese who had made good, representing a powerful U.S. senator named David Boren.

So my hosts liked me, especially when I made small talk with them in Mandarin. ("Your pronunciation is so good!" they would say, meaning, perhaps, that my grammar and vocabulary left something to be desired.) I liked them too. But I kept my distance. In our meetings, after the obligatory statements of Sino-American goodwill, I would clearly enunciate my boss's concerns about China's human rights record. I didn't want our time with the power brokers to devolve into mere "friendship and understanding" sessions. At the same time, I tried to speak with care and tact, without grandstanding. And I think they respected that. *This is someone we can do business with,* I felt them thinking. By the end of the weeklong visit, the vice foreign minister had invited me to join him for a private lunch.

When I met him and his interpreter at the restaurant the next day, I got the odd feeling that we were all doing this just to be polite. The vice minister was preoccupied with other matters. He held his chopsticks lazily and hardly ate. He kept a formal mien, which made me think he might have an important message to convey to the senator: maybe a dissident would soon be released, or a major trading contract announced. But he had no such message; he was just being formal. After a while the lunch ended. All in all, it had been something of a dud. And yet, this was one of the most thrilling moments of my youthful career in government. For I realized then that perhaps one day I might serve as a builder of bridges between America and China, the two great powers of my time.

A friend of my in-laws, a dry fellow with a dramatic flair, predicted upon meeting me that this would be my destiny. He was certain of it. Well, I'm a sucker both for flattery and for talk of personal destiny, so I rolled that one around like a hard candy: *Eric Liu, Pacific bridge-builder, Man of Peace.* Mmmmm. When I think about it more seriously, though, I'm not sure I'd want that fate. I'm not sure I would want to be a middleman, a mediator, in disputes political or commercial. Embedded in that role, it seems to me, is the presumption that as a Chinese American I am a bit of each but not a lot of either. That I belong to no side. Such are the perils of a go-between identity: moral agnosticism, self-imposed exile.

What I *would* want to be is, oh, say, the U.S. ambassador to China. Now, that's a role I'd relish: representing my nation, its interests, its values. Of course, that seems like such a distant dream—not only for me, but for Chinese Americans in general. Though plenty of Americans have served as ambassadors to their ancestral homelands—we have today a Kennedy in Ireland—it is still difficult to imagine a Chinese American envoy to China. Maybe that's because there aren't many Chinese Americans in the main feeding pools for ambassadorial positions—Congress, the Foreign Service, the ranks of big campaign donors (ha!). Or maybe it's because such a person would *look* to some people as if she wasn't quite on our side. For the time being, it would seem, this bridge remains a bridge too far.

War

When I was in the third grade I dreamed of killing Japs.

Perhaps I should elaborate. When I was in the third grade I became an avid student of World War II. I built model warplanes. I learned the insignia of every branch of the armed services. I devoured accounts of the decisive battles. I devotedly watched a TV series called *Baa Baa Black Sheep*, about a squadron of daredevil marine fighter pilots in the Pacific theater. And as I lay in bed at night, I would imagine that I was one of them, a young ace in the cockpit of my own gull-winged Corsair, chasing a quick, silvery Japanese Zero through the skies over Guadalcanal.

It was a great fantasy. Abetting it was the fact that my own grandfather had been a pilot, and eventually a general, in the Nationalist Chinese air force. He'd tangled with the Japanese for over a decade. Even better, he had worked with General Chennault and the other Americans to help launch the Flying Tigers program. As a Chinese American, then, I'd been born twice into the camp of the good guys. To celebrate this, I penned a collection of breathless one-page stories, "Tigers, Zeroes and Corsairs," in which Chinese and American pilots joined forces, in dogfight after victorious dogfight, against the dastardly Japs.

Recently, I unearthed those short stories and read them again. I was braced, frankly, for a few embarrassing snatches of anti-Japanese dialogue, picked up from the many war movies I'd seen. To my relief, the tales focused earnestly on the mechanics of battle: the time, the place, the number of aircraft, the intricate patterns of combat. And to my surprise, whenever I talked about the "Japs," I did it just like that—with scare quotes. As if to distance myself from the usage. Did my younger self somehow know that "Japs" was an odd thing for a nice Chinese boy to be saying?

I doubt it. I was only a boy, after all. I wasn't particularly sensitive to such things. A measure of my insensitivity, indeed, is that in the midst of all my elaborate daydreaming, one rather basic question always managed to elude me: What if my grandfather had fought *against* the Americans instead of alongside them? Never, really, did I wonder what it must have been like to be a Japanese American boy during the war—or forty years after the war—and to realize that my ancestral homeland was on the wrong side of history. Not once did I ask myself: What if China was the enemy?

These days, the question crosses my mind a bit more. I don't mean to suggest that China and America are headed for war, or that conflict is even likely. I worry, in fact, that such prophecies of hostility can be self-fulfilling. Still, there's no doubt that the emergence of China in recent years—as an economic dynamo, as a military power, as a global counterweight to the United States—has got plenty of Americans jittery. For the first time, I've had occasion to imagine even the distant possibility that the Chinese people could one day be a direct threat to the interests, even the survival, of my nation.

What I would do in the event of war is hard to imagine. I would fight if called. I don't know, however, whether I would be moved to volunteer. If it came to a situation where Chinese Americans were being officially ostracized on account of their heritage, I'd like to think that I would be vocal in my resistance. Of course, that's easy for me to say today. As much as I admire those Japanese Americans who fought for their country by forming the all-Nisei 442nd Regiment after Pearl Harbor, so do I admire those who fought for their country by suing a government that had wrongfully imprisoned them. Would I have had the courage to do either? I like to think so. But that knowledge, alas, cannot be gotten on the cheap.

Glory

Around the time that Hong Kong became Chinese again, my mother said she was proud that China is no longer weak. I can't say I feel exactly that way. I suppose I prefer a strong

China to one that is a plaything for colonial powers. But what would make me truly proud is if China became a liberal democracy: more like America. That, perhaps, is the difference between the first and second generations.

I am friends with a woman who, it is hard to believe, was one of the student leaders in Tiananmen Square in 1989. It is hard to believe not because of her temperament—she is determined, strong—but because she is so Americanized on the surface. She has lived here since 1990 or so; has learned to speak nearly flawless English; has earned degrees from Ivy League schools; has worked for a consulting firm; has picked up the aura of a young professional. And yet, unlike my mother, she still may harbor dreams of returning to China one day. That is the difference between the immigrant and the expatriate.

The other day I saw a grown man wearing a T-shirt proclaiming SERBIAN PRIDE. There was a coat of arms and some medieval lettering, but the design was clearly American. I was embarrassed for him. And not just because of Bosnia. You see, I'm not likely ever to wear a T-shirt that says CHINESE PRIDE. I don't feel comfortable with the idea of, say, a "Kiss Me—I'm Chinese" button. I can't imagine a Chinese counterpart to the Saint Patrick's Day parade in Boston. That is the difference between the assimilated and the assimilating.

Let China grow strong, then; let its power run wide. And let Chinese Americans, and all Asian Americans, bask in the glow of a billion confident yellow people with five thousand years of history behind them. But let us recall, too, that what matters in the end is not one's inheritance but what one makes of it. That is the difference between glory reflected and glory.

The Ugly Chinese

In Beijing they have debates now, in restaurants and bars and classrooms, about how Western—how American, that is— China should allow itself to become. Among certain young people it has become fashionable to spout a defiant anti-American nationalism. Of course, it has also become fashionable to wear Levi's and follow the NBA and watch MTV and smoke Marlboros. In Taiwan, meanwhile, the writer Bo Yang has ruffled feathers for years with a satirical tract called *The Ugly Chinese*, calling on the Chinese to abandon the Confucian narrowness of their character and, in some respects, to emulate the West.

In America we can't quite bring ourselves to have such a debate, at least not in such open and plain terms. How Chinese should we become? How Asian? We prefer to sublimate our identity crises, to express them through paroxysm. We prefer, in our politics and literature and mythologies, to hang on to a prelapsarian dream of pure identity. We prefer to think of the nation as white, European, until confronted by hard evidence to the contrary. Then we prefer to scare ourselves with hallucinations of invasion or contagion, with overwrought visions of an unstoppable clash of civilizations. *The West versus the Rest.*

Everywhere the frontiers are dissolving, history is spilling forth, and yet we still persist in excluding Asians: not from our territory anymore but from that region of our mind where the nation truly begins. This is madness. Today, for the first time in centuries, Asia is awakening to the breadth of its potential. It is time that America did too.

New
Jews

Some of my best friends are Jewish. Really. Why that is, I'm not sure. But it's fitting, I think, considering how often I myself am called a Jew.

Over the last few years, Asian Americans have come to be known as the New Jews. The label is an honorific. It is meant to accentuate the many parallels between these two groups of immigrants-made-good: Jews started out as outsiders; Asians did too. Jews dedicated themselves to schooling; Asians too. Jews climbed the barriers and crowded the Ivies; Asians too. Jews climbed faster than any other minority in their time; Asians too. Jews enjoy Chinese food; Asians—well, you get the picture. Somewhere in that half-lit region between stereotype and sociology, the notion has taken hold that Asian Americans are "out-Jewing the Jews."

Usually it is Old Jews who remark upon this phenomenon. And well they should. It is a remarkable thing that there could be New Jews. For what it means is not merely that the Old Jews have assimilated. It means also that here in America, the very metaphor of "the Jew" now stands for assimilation.

———

Who shall be a Jew?

Whosoever shall arrive at these shores and be regarded as a sojourner, an alien, beyond the pale; whosoever shall resort to clannish ways and strange methods to promote his kind and find, by dint of unseemly ambition, that he exercises influence in this society far out of proportion; whosoever shall, by negation, remind his countrymen of what it means to be a countryman, to belong; whosoever shall alter the very flavor of the society that swallows him; whosoever shall do all these things without meaning to do anything but live by a creed that will, in the end, spell his brilliant unmaking: he, too, shall be a Jew.

———

I remember my first Passover Seder. There were five of us: two Asians, two Jews, and a Pole. (This is not a joke.) My friends Lauren and Jill led the ceremony, explained the meaning of each step. I was so struck by the beauty of it all. And the portability. It was as if I were back in grade school, earnestly learning the lessons of another culture. I took very seriously the theme of remembrance, though I couldn't tell you now how to hold a Seder. I do recall that we giggled as we bid each other "Next year in Jerusalem."

———

As it happened, the next year I *was* in Jerusalem, on a business trip. I was walking through the Old City, and our tour guide, an American turned Israeli, was walking silently beside me. Ahead of us were a few others from my group, joking, high-fiving. *Your family is . . . ?* the guide asked me suddenly. *Chinese,* I replied, deducing the arc of his ellipse. He smiled. *So you know what it's like to belong to an ancient people. There's history in our bones.* He tapped his forearm for emphasis. I smiled back.

Another ritual meal: my mother and my wife and I, together in Boston, spend Thanksgiving with the Greenbergs. David is a friend of mine, his parents have invited us to join them. There is turkey, cranberry sauce, pie. We've brought a Chinese dish my mother created, fried tofu with snow peas and mushrooms. It is eaten up heartily, complimented, forgotten by the second serving of mashed potatoes. The Greenbergs couldn't be more warm and welcoming. But I feel we are intruding. David's sister is to be married soon; her fiancé is there, in a dark suit. David and his brother have brought their girlfriends. This is a family. David's father gracefully adapts his toast to include us, the guests.

Not long ago, *The New York Times* ran a series of advertisements in the lower right corner of the op-ed page. The ads, written as first-person columns, were sponsored by the American Jewish Committee. Their theme was "What Being Jewish

Means to Me." In each one, a prominent Jew recounted how heritage and faith had shaped his or her values and formed a lasting foundation for success. The text was always intriguing. The subtext, even more so.

It seems to me that being Jewish today means, in no small measure, having the ability to run ads in *The New York Times* about what being Jewish today means. The public introspection of very public figures—a Supreme Court justice, an astronaut, a university president, a Nobel Prize winner—is at once an announcement of having made it and an assertion that Jewishness did not prevent them from making it.

At the same time, one can read these ads as an appeal to the younger generation: as an effort to stop the exodus of the heart, the rescattering of the Jews by assimilation. In this light, the ads seem more doleful. They convey nearly as much doubt as confidence.

We should all have so much doubt. Can you imagine a series in the *Times* called "What Being Chinese Means to Me"? Sure, there would be prominent people to showcase, and they'd have thoughtful things to say. But it is a question of concept: Chinese Americans do not imagine themselves a single entity whose voice should fit seamlessly into the daily digest of elite opinion. And yet neither could I imagine a series called "What Being a WASP Means to Me." Somehow, that would seem unnecessary, even unseemly. It is, then, the mark of a particular moment both to have the podium and to be trumpeting one's accomplishment as *ethnic*: it is an epitaph, a farewell to the days of ever proving oneself.

———

I suggest to a friend that the difference between "her people" and "mine" is that Jews have a tangible history, a unified cultural inheritance that they can draw from in their everyday lives. What, by contrast, do Asians have? My friend frowns. "The difference you're talking about isn't the difference between Asians and Jews; it's the difference between you and me," she says. "If I were Chinese, I'd be turning to Confucius and Chinese history and looking for all the ways that they'd shaped me."

Of course, Confucianism is not a religious faith like Judaism: that distinction is critical. But my friend has a point. It's too easy to complain that there is no pan-ethnic "Asian" heritage or tradition to draw from. For certainly there exists a *Chinese* heritage, one that a Chinese American may either embrace or ignore. One that can be sustained. It is only a matter of wanting to sustain it, wanting to seek out the connections. Thus far in my life, I have not felt that want very strongly.

In college I took a course called "The Search for Modern China," taught by the historian Jonathan Spence. I bought *The Analects*, by Confucius. This was the first time I had encountered the work of the great sage. I read intently, breaking the spine of the book, folding page corners, underlining apt passages. But nothing sank in, really. I felt I was reading a distillation of something quite undistillable, the Cliffs Notes of Chinese morality. The words I understood. The meaning, I'd say, escaped me.

Part of it, perhaps, was that I was reading an English edition. Not that I could have read the original Chinese. But I know enough to know that the difference matters. In English, a line like "The Master said, 'Unbending strength, resoluteness, simplicity and reticence are close to benevolence'" comes off like a parody of fortune-cookie philosophy. In Chinese, in the setting of a Chinese text, such a line can draw force from its imprecision. There is less connective tissue in a Chinese sentence. There is thus something more compact and expressive about a Chinese word. That something can get lost in the translation.

In any language, of course, *The Analects* can turn into an inkblot or a Ouija board. Max Weber blamed Confucianism for the pitiful backwardness of nineteenth-century China. Today, business gurus credit it for China's economic boom. Singapore's longtime leader Lee Kuan Yew, Anglophile turned "Asian values" cheerleader, sees in The Master's teachings a prescription for heavy-handed authoritarian politics. Tu Wei-Ming, a Harvard Confucian scholar, finds in *The Analects* evidence of a tolerant, humanist philosophy. I am reminded of that odd work of verbal numerology *The Bible Code*. We see what we like in an ancient book; the words spell out what lessons we search for.

So it is, I fear, with the notions of "racial character" that come attached like barnacles to any great ethnic heritage. My friend assessed me well. I am deeply skeptical that *The Analects* or the *Tao Te-Ching* worked their way into my cultural DNA; if I were Jewish, I'd likely be just as skeptical of the Torah and Talmud. Talk of racial character, of a racial way of thinking and being, simply makes me nervous.

But why, exactly? Why such a reflex of suspicion? Every generation passes down certain messages to the next. And that code, even if unspoken, is transmitted through a distinct cultural medium. My father believed that his ethical sense and inner equilibrium derived in great measure from his boyhood reading of the Chinese classics. I don't doubt his assessment. Nor do I doubt how much my own ethical sense derives from his. So while he never schooled me in the Chinese classics, does that mean I didn't learn from them?

Perhaps when I protest that Chineseness is a mere mirage, I protest too much. Perhaps there *is* a there there. Someday, when a child of mine dares me to look, perhaps I will find it.

Like many in the second generation, I suffer from an affliction called "memory-envy."

We inherit memory, some of us more than others. I have, of course, my precious store of personal family remembrances: recollections from my twenty-nine years, with an appendix of images and captions that unfolds backward in time and stops abruptly after two generations. But I don't have anything like communal memory, the sense that my life is the latest page in the history of a *race*. *World of Our Fathers* is what Irving Howe called his great tome on the Jewish migrations from Eastern Europe to America. I would never presume to give a book of mine such a title. I do not have the confidence; I do not have the sort of meta-memory—the memory of memory—that pulls individuals into a tribe.

And I envy those who do. Lori Hope Lefkovitz writes in *The Kenyon Review* that "We [Jews] maintain the legend that all of us were present for the giving of the law at Sinai, the dead and the yet-to-be-born alike. And when we remember the Exodus at the Passover Seder, we not only commemorate a liberation from slavery in ancient Egypt but we perform an annual ritual reenactment of our own liberation, commanded as we are to regard ourselves as members of the original generation that was saved by divine intervention in history."

These words beguile me. *The dead and the yet-to-be-born alike* . . . My only notion of this is literal: I will want my father to be knowable to my children. But toward the innumerable Chinese of past and future—the Long Yellow Line—I feel no real affinity . . . *commanded as we are* . . . I do not feel commanded at all; the absence of history's command was the essence of my upbringing . . . *the original generation* . . . This is not some ancient touchstone; it is me. I am the first in my family to be born American.

152

Lefkowitz writes about being a child of Holocaust sur-
vivors. She tells of being in a strange position: the keeper, the
speaker, of other people's memories. A ventriloquist. She
writes of the Jews as a community of memory.

Of course, even the Jews, especially younger ones, have
begun to forget: not the Holocaust, but the heritage that pre-
dated and survived the Holocaust. Patterns of ritual and
meaning are falling away: dietary laws, Sabbath candles. Intermarriage has produced an identity crisis, spawned a generation
that might prove to be Jewish mainly in the way that Italians
are Italian.

The assimilationist instinct—my instinct, at times—is to
sand away difference, to aspire to a hairless, skinless, bloodless
universalism. But it occurs to me, as I consider the entry of the
Jews into the American ethnoscape, that nothing becomes universal unless it is first particular. And it occurs to me that I have
never really been grounded so: in a historical tradition, or a
faith; in the rites of an ageless culture.

A winter afternoon in Seattle. Shawn Wong, the pioneer-
ing Asian American novelist, listens patiently as I sit in his
office and sing my paean to race transcendence. If he thinks
me callow, his face does not betray it. Only after I have delivered my monologue does he warn me, gently, not to forget history. By which he means Asian American history: the trials of
people before my time, whose estrangement from the mainstream years ago made possible my entry into the mainstream

today. I realize, yes, I should know better the origins of my own situation. And I think, here in this narrative is a source of belonging. But then I wonder: Should I stop with Asian American stories? Should I even begin there?

It became my peculiar specialty, when I was a speechwriter for President Clinton, to compose memorial speeches. A requiem for the Pan Am 103 victims in Lockerbie. A eulogy for servicemen killed on a mission of mercy to the Iraqi Kurds. And most memorably, a fiftieth-anniversary tribute to the heroes of D-Day, delivered at the American cemetery in Normandy. On the day of that address, in the presence of the old veterans who still lived, my memory-envy cased a bit. Welling in my eyes, catching in my throat, was a *nation's* memory, a public history: something that I, too, could claim.

One reason why I could relate to my Jewish friends when I was a boy was that they were the only other kids I knew whose parents made them get an ethnic education. And they, like me, did their best to stifle the enterprise with inattention. Their schooling was on Thursday nights, mine on Sunday afternoons. Hebrew school, from what I could gather, was most notably a social scene, a place where flirtations and intrigue from the regular school day could further develop. Certainly these kids learned *something* in their classes; at least, they always managed to perform well enough at their bar and bat mitzvahs. But their hearts weren't really in it. Many of them had learned that the appearance of observance was as important as observance itself; that religion could be reduced to mechanical obligation.

Chinese school was only three hours a week, but it too felt like an endless chore. I can still see the angle of autumn sunshine, the mournful light of lost playtime, as my parents took me to the middle school that the Chinese Association rented on Sundays. I was a good student, respectful, but what I recall now are only the things that distracted me: someone's notebook left in the desk; a line of loopy cursive on the blackboard; the drone of children reading Chinese in slow unison; the inky smell of the freshly mimeographed grid paper on which we practiced writing characters; the way we rolled that paper into cone-shaped containers for the corn chips the teacher brought; the aloof eyes of the janitor who opened and closed the building for us. One year Dad was the principal and Mom was one of the teachers. We had a great Chinese New Year party that winter. Somebody brought a boxful of hot McDonald's hamburgers.

Given my experience, I'd guess that such schools are fated to disappear in the next generation. But then, these things ebb and flow. On the heels of a recent (and inaccurate) study that showed Jews marrying outside the faith at a rate of over 50 percent come reports now that enrollment in Jewish private schools is surging nationwide. Granted, these are full-time schools, not once-a-week supplements, and many are run by Orthodox Jews, not by the more secular likes of my childhood neighbors. Still, the emergence of these institutions, ranging from yeshivas to college prep academies, suggests that the future of Jewish identity in America isn't necessarily a steady dwindling down to zero. Another generation is still learning.

In the Washington suburbs where my mother now lives, the weekly Chinese schools are thriving as well. From time to time Mom will drop by the noisy public school gymnasium in Rockville that serves as a Chinese center on weekends. On one side of the gym, kids of many ages play volleyball and basketball. On the other side, parents have set up a table to sell homemade dumplings and other foods. In rooms down the hall are Chinese-language classes, *qigong* classes, calligraphy classes. Minivans crowd the parking lot. This is more than a school. It is a home base. It is an oasis, a refuge from the fierce, leveling winds of assimilation. My mother likes it here. It's too bad, she says, there was never anything so well developed, so comfortably Chinese, back home.

Whoever the New Asians are in the next century—or will they be New New Jews?—they will first make themselves known in the classroom.

It was in the classroom that Jewish students two and three generations ago worked with feverish intensity, captured the highest prizes, filled the honor rolls. It was in the classroom that a rumor began to circulate: a rumor of Jewish superiority, Jewish smarts. It was in the classroom too that non-Jews learned to contain that rumor, to preserve the order of things, by reducing Jewish smarts to mere "cleverness."

They are imitative. They have a tendency for memorization. They work like machines. So said the deans of Columbia and Harvard of the Jews who were "overrunning" their campuses in the 1920s and 1930s. The Asian today, like the Jew before him, is said to be a grind. A single-minded, relentless automaton. This is how he became known to his countrymen in the 1980s: as the whiz kid and nerd. *Not well rounded. Not cultivated. Rote-minded; not dedicated to learning for its own sake.* Just as Jews once faced college admission quotas, so, it is believed, have Asians.

The Asian today, like the Jew before him, is said to be too hungry. In his memoir *Making It,* Norman Podhoretz tells of migrating from the Lower East Side to Columbia in the 1950s: an earnest Jewish boy hungry for knowledge, eager to show his stuff, who finds once there that the prevailing mode of courtly WASP gentility makes him seem *all wrong.* Today Asian kids are the ones who strive, grasp, and stick in the culture's craw because of their unabashed ambition. Rather than acting like normal kids—slacker-athletes—Asian Americans are seen as pressing an unfair advantage. They are "overachieving." Which raises the question: Over what? Over whose expectations? What unseen ceilings?

One way to explain the abnormal ambition of a group is to racialize it. Hard work and sacrifice? Deferral of gratification? Devotion to education? Today, anyone will tell you, these are "Asian values." But remember, only a few generations ago they were "Jewish values." And once upon a time, of course, they were "Protestant values."

This is tricky territory to navigate. In today's coded conversations about race, rumors of *inherent* Asian superiority can feed rumors of *inherent* black inferiority. This helps explain why some Asian American activists go to great lengths to remind people how troubled their community actually is, how riddled with shortcomings and social pathology. They treat praise as damnation, commendation as calumny.

Certainly there is something condescending—and misleading—about the "model minority" label. But when an Asian American student does well she should be able to take credit for her diligence without feeling that she's playing into a devious plot to dehumanize her and all colored people. She should be able to say that virtue has its rewards.

She should also, however, give credit where it is due: to circumstance. Stephen Steinberg, a City University sociologist, reminds us in *The Ethnic Myth* that for Jews and Asians alike, many in the first generation arrived with considerable built-in advantages of class, education, and expectations. It is this social capital, and the selectivity of the immigration itself, that has helped both groups achieve here.

My own story suggests this. I've always had the desire to do well, and the dedication, but I have also been fortunate. My father and mother were professionals. They had come here not to scrape out a living but to attend university. There was never any question that I would go to college, never any doubt that they'd send me wherever I chose to go. When I was a boy and my cousin went to Yale, it seemed only natural that I should set my sights as high.

I was fortunate another way: my father and mother never pressured me. In this regard, I realize, they were atypical. I've known those legendary Chinese parents who forced their kids to do x hours of homework and y hours of violin and z hours of SAT prep every day. Not Mom and Dad. They were, in truth, more laissez-faire than even I might be as a parent. I worked hard enough, was curious and obsessive enough to pursue interests like music, but I also goofed off more than most Chinese kids I knew. I played more baseball, built more forts, watched more television, ate more junk food, spent more time at the video arcade.

There are sociological studies showing that second-generation Chinese and Japanese American children tend to assimilate downward. Compared with first-generation children, that is, they have lower test scores, more indifferent attitudes toward school. By the time you get to the third generation, the academic profile becomes roughly comparable to that of whites: average. What is going on here is not just that the Asian American child picks up bad habits; it is that she perceives that something else matters.

I formed my sense of self at school—by being smart and getting high marks, but also, as I became old enough to care, by finding ways not to appear like a geek. One way was for me and my gang to fancy ourselves "wildmen": to say cheeky things to our teachers, to stage gags in class, and, after school, to do ill-considered things like make flamethrowers and engage in car chases down wet country roads.

Another way was to find a geek of my own. I did. She was Indian, less assimilated, with a trace of an accent. She was a hard-core student: private, humorless, apparently friendless. She scored near the top on every test, but, well . . . *she was not well rounded; not cultivated; she was rote-minded.* With jealous insecurity we mocked her (behind her back, although to her face we weren't very nice either). I'm not proud of this. I imagine that in another school, I would have been her. I imagine, indeed, that to some of my own schoolmates, she and I were indistinguishable: Asian nerds.

What else did I learn in school? I learned, or at least began to limn, the limits of meritocracy. I learned about cultural bias—not of standardized tests like the SAT, but of the world beyond SATs. During the summer after tenth grade I and two of my friends (both Jewish) went to Phillips Andover Academy, the preppy private school outside Boston. That eight-week summer session was revelatory. The academic expectations were college-level, far higher than what I was used to. The breadth of interests and pursuits among my classmates was staggering. But more important, this was my first encounter with young privileged WASPs, and with Jews and Asians and blacks who moved with the same easy air of entitlement— sometimes decadence—as young privileged WASPs.

I had an awful time the first week. I was way out of my element. Then I fell in with a group of fellow exiles: an air force brat, a valley dude, a Belgian, a Japanese, a Brooklyn kid. We became fast friends, and from the safe haven of our friendship I ventured out to explore this strange realm that grades and test scores could not explain. The idiom at Andover was Anglo: brick buildings with Mayflower names, neatly trimmed quadrangles. But the style was something else now. There was a way of being among these kids, Gentiles and Jews alike, that suggested everybody already knew everybody else. I felt like a visitor to the future. It seemed as if I were among my own children or their children: those well past counting the generations; those who, for better and worse, won't really have to earn it.

When I came back to school that fall, the classroom seemed beside the point.

———

There was a time, only a few decades ago, when every WASP and every Negro knew that the Jew was something else, a third thing. At that moment, Jews were in transition: partly accepted, partly stigmatized; half in, half out. Then, with the war and the suburbs and the fifties and the sixties, something happened: the Jews became white. Today, many Asian Americans seem to be in a similar position. Thus I am told sometimes, with an implied pat on the back, that Asians are now "graduating" from minority status.

It is an odd notion, *graduating*. Implied is the idea that minority status is a junior stage of Americanness. Implied also is the idea that you don't have to have white skin anymore to become white. All you need is not to be a *special pleader*, a *whiny victim*, a *racial claimant*. At work here is a schema, a crude model, in which people are deemed either "white" (in power, self-sufficient) or "minority" (in opposition, dependent). The trouble is, Asian Americans, the so-called model minority, don't fit this minority model.

Consider affirmative action. In the quantum mechanics of identity, Asian Americans occupy an unstable position between ethnicity and race. In certain contexts they are perceived in terms of the old European immigrants, "new Jews" who will enter the mainstream like the "other" white ethnics. In other contexts they are a distinct race, a group of nonwhites. Conservatives, in their assault on racial preferences, like to trot out hardworking, play-by-the-rules Asian immigrants as the true victims of racial "quotas." Liberals react by cramming Asians into a rhetorical framework of resistance, built for blacks and recast for "people of color." Neither usage feels correct to me.

Do Asian Americans need affirmative action? It depends, actually, on what you mean by "Asian Americans" and by "affirmative action." There are plenty of well-educated second-generation Asian Americans like myself who can meet the numerical criteria (sometimes called "strict merit") required for entry to Yale or Berkeley. On that basis you might say that affirmative action—defined as admission preferences—hurts Asians, since it creates slots for other people who don't have the right numbers (including, by the way, many white children of alumni).

But many of the Asian Americans who insist on "strict merit" may find that something else determines their ascent in the world beyond Yale and Berkeley. Stanley Kaplan does not teach you how to break glass ceilings or equalize pay scales. Affirmative action—defined as recruitment and mentoring— can thus be an imperfect corrective to a system suffused with the bias of "who you know." Meanwhile there are many other Asian Americans, more recent arrivals with fewer resources and more troubled lives, with a higher incidence of crime and poverty, for whom higher education seems a distant dream and for whom the workplace can be unremittingly hostile. For this overlooked and growing segment of Asian America the debates about corporate and college affirmative action programs can seem rather inconsequential.

The debates, in a way, *are* inconsequential now. In legislatures and courtrooms across the land, the right wing's vision of a magical, self-executing regime of color blindness is prevailing. Many on the left bemoan or even deny this state of affairs. I would rather take it as an opportunity: to call the color-blind absolutists on the disingenuousness of their vision; and to begin again, with tools more targeted to the youngest and least advantaged, at the work of leveling the field. That work remains necessary. For even after the age of affirmative action, the minority model still has too great a hold on the American imagination.

Chutzpah!

I am sitting across a cluttered desk from Alan Dershowitz. He is talking about "thinking Jewishly," about how "as a Jew," he has a competitive advantage in lawyering because of the great Jewish tradition of argumentation. He is not the cartoon figure I expected—far from it. He is subtle, engaging, attentive. "I was like you when I was your age," he says. "I didn't make a big deal about being Jewish." But I realize that when he was my age, he was getting rejected from every WASP law firm he'd applied to for a summer job—even though he was editor of the law review and headed for a Supreme Court clerkship. What's *my* excuse? What's keeping *me* from wearing my heritage on my sleeve?

I struggle to find, in all the American vernacular, a Chinese contribution as significant as chutzpah. Embodied in this word is an attitude, a defanged stereotype, a nutshell explana-

tion for the great success of the Jews. True, there are still settings where it's not wise to be, as the title of a recent art exhibit
put it, "Too Jewish." But a society where everyone knows and
values chutzpah is already quite Jewish.

By contrast, perhaps the most recognizable, if most misun-
derstood, aspect of the Chinese cultural style is the idea of
"face": saving face, losing face. Face, actually, is the exact
inverse of chutzpah. It is about smoothing things over, eliding
confrontation, not forcing the issue. Will this subtle art be the
Chinese way of shaping the American personality? A study in
the *Journal of Applied Behavioral Science* suggests that the
Asian style of "impression management" gives whites the false
impression that Asian employees aren't fit for leadership. If you
ask some first-generation Chinese Americans in private, they'll
tell you that the Chinese could stand being more like the Jews:
more *lihai,* more assertive.

I think of my mother. When I told her about Alan Dershowitz, she uttered the universal misgivings of the first generation: *He shouldn't say so much.* But it is also my mother who
believes the Chinese need to speak out more, especially amid
the anti-Asian undertones of the campaign-finance scandals.
My mother is brave: she will stand up in any gathering, all-
Chinese or no-Chinese, to say her piece.

I think of J. D. Hokoyama, a third-generation Japanese
American in Los Angeles who founded LEAP: Leadership
Education for Asian Pacifics. LEAP provides, among other

things, diversity training for corporations—teaching managers to unlearn the assumption that if an Asian employee is quiet she has nothing to offer. It also provides assertiveness training—teaching the employee to make her voice known.

I think of a Vietnamese medical student my wife knows, a twenty-three-year-old immigrant who cannot stop asking questions. She asks the residents, the attendings, her fellow third-years. She asks about medicine, about the weather, about the news, anything. She is indiscriminate, fearless, sometimes senseless in her asking. I have to wonder: is it nature or is it nurture that sends the questions spilling forth?

I think of me, gung ho, ever eager to show that Asians aren't meek. I am overconditioned. Once, in officer candidates school, my platoon commander pulled me aside. "I notice," he said, "that when you give an order you deepen your voice." I blinked, not realizing this. "You don't need to," he said. "Just speak naturally."

As late as 1974 a prominent Jewish commentator could lament that Jews did not run for office more frequently because of their "ghetto mentality" and "feeling of limited expectations and vulnerability." But that very year, notes J. J. Goldberg in his provocative study *Jewish Power*, a new era began. The post-Watergate class of 1974 nearly doubled the number of Jews in the House of Representatives. Since then, the Congress has had a Jewish membership of somewhere between 8 and 10 percent. And no one accuses Jews today of timidity in politics.

Asian Americans—well, that is a different story. Consider that between 1976 and 1996, California's Asian American population quadrupled to more than four million—transforming the state's schools, workplaces, and neighborhoods. During that same period, the Asian American presence in the California legislature doubled—from one legislator to two. There are now almost ten million Asian Americans across the country; there are only five voting Asian American members of the House and Senate.

Over the years, many reasons have been offered for this power gap, most of which boil down to "ghetto mentality" and "feelings of limited expectation and vulnerability." It seems to me, though, that demographics are critical here: the Asian American community, after all, is still a community of immigrants—two thirds foreign-born. It seems as well that time and acculturation will narrow the gap. Indeed, Don Nakanishi, director of UCLA's Asian Americans Studies Center, reports that record numbers of Asian Americans entered politics in 1996 as candidates, staffers, voters, and, of course, donors.

What have been the consequences so far? A cynic might scoff that Asian Americans, once ciphers, have simply emerged as pawns. Which is to say, they have ascended from near-total political irrelevance to a narrowly circumscribed usefulness. In previous elections they became useful as a bipartisan fountain of cash. Now that their money and motives are seen as suspect, they are useful in new ways—as metonyms for malfeasance, stand-ins for a diseased campaign-finance regime.

But the cynic's view is only partly right—the yin, as some have observed, to a sunnier yang. And if John Huang represents the shadier side of Asian American political ambition, a man named Gary Locke embodies its more promising aspects. Locke was elected Washington State's governor in 1996, becoming the nation's first Chinese American governor and the first Asian American governor on the mainland. He grew up in a Seattle housing project, worked in his father's grocery, went to Yale on scholarship. After law school, he spent a career in public life. The statehouse he now occupies is but a mile from the dwelling where his grandfather once worked as a houseboy.

The arrival of an all-American figure like Locke has awakened Asian American hopes. And it raises all the big questions of ethnic politics: Should Asian Americans try to act as a voting bloc? The "community" remains divided in significant ways—by class, ethnicity, language, ideology. But the GOP's hard line on immigration, like its opposition to the nomination of Bill Lann Lee to be assistant attorney general, has pushed many Asian Americans into politics (and toward the Democrats).

What special obligations, if any, attach to the Asian American politician? Should she focus on "Asian" issues? Help build Asian organizations? Some Jewish politicians are politicians who happen to be Jewish while others, in Goldberg's formulation, are *"Jewish" Jewish politicians*. Can an Asian American politician afford to be an Asian Asian politician?

Increasingly, yes. For now, there are only a few Asian American figures on the national scene, people like Locke or Robert Matsui, the longtime U.S. congressman from California. But as more leaders of Asian descent stride into the public square, each of them—and each of us—will have progressively more freedom of movement in politics: freedom to speak for one's race, to speak for oneself, or both.

In his essay "Jews in Second Place," Nicholas Lemann writes of the secret vice of "Jew-counting." He is watching his son play in a hockey league, reflecting on the days when Jewish nerds didn't play *goyim* sports. On the ice he counts all the "little Cohens, little Levys, their names sewn in block letters on the backs of their jerseys." He realizes that Asians have replaced Jews atop the meritocracy.

There is something deliciously irresistible about ethnic counting. How many names belong to my kind? Who here stands in for me? Which of these are *mine*? Of course, to a Jew, "Jew-counting" is probably most satisfying not in the roster of preteen hockey leagues but in the roll call of Congress, the Forbes 400, the mastheads of the media, the top of the film credits, the register of university presidents.

It might surprise you to learn that Jews constitute only 2 percent of the population: the figure seems low. It might also surprise you that Asians constitute 4 percent: the figure, by comparison, seems high.

Maybe we're hardwired to sort by groups. But in our contemporary swirl of blood, genes, and culture, this bit of evolutionary instinct is beginning to run out its usefulness. What's in a name today? What, exactly, does "Kim" signify? What mysteries are embedded in "Rubin"? How reliable a guide is "Lee"? (I refer you to the episode of *Seinfeld* in which Jerry's image of a woman named Donna Chang disintegrates when it turns out she's Donna Changstein, from Long Island.)

It is worth remembering too that other people count and notice the names. Recall the way that Pat Buchanan, in an inflammatory stump speech, stretched out the Jewishness of "Ruuuth Ba-der Ginsbuuurg" with a stomach-turning sneer. Recall Ross Perot's complaint as he scanned a list of Asian American Democratic Party donors: "You know, so far we haven't found an American name."

Recall the reports that Charlie Trie and Johnny Chung entered the White House thirty-six times, or fifty-eight, or a thousand-and-one, or whatever. It sounds like a lot. But it sounds that way in part because you never hear how many times other people get access to the White House. You also never hear about the Asian Americans who've been *denied* access because the Secret Service assumed they were foreigners.

For Asian Americans today, the counting of names can still be a metaphor for conspicuity. But remember: conspicuity is in the eye of the beholder. There used to be a time when Jewish names stuck out, when little Cohens and little Levys would have been chased off the ice. Times changed. Jew-counting is still a *secret* vice because Jews remember the malign purposes that Jew-counting once served. But Jewish "overrepresentation" in the power structure no longer seems very notable, let alone alarming. We have no doubt but that their names are American, among the most American of American.

It won't be long, I hope, before the same can be said of Asian names. I'm counting the days.

———

The Jews assimilated, we know: became American. But America assimilated too: became Jewish. You could write a book about the Jewish influence on the cultural and social idiom, but then, you would only be writing a book about twentieth-century America.

A novelist from England speaks of "the Great Jews" — Bellow, Malamud, Roth, and so on — who articulated the inner life of midcentury America. It was a Jewish playwright named Israel Zangwill who immortalized the phrase "the melting pot." And what was Hollywood, asks author Neal Gabler, but the invention of Jews who wanted so badly to invent another America? Listen now to television, or the radio, or a conversation on the bus: the Jews gave us another voice. *What, you need an example?* The Jew changed the very inflection of an American question. The Jew changed our food, our images, our language, our humor, our law, our literature.

The Asian, so far, has changed our food.

I understate, yes. American culture is Asian in ways we don't even think twice about now: feng shui and Ayurvedic healing and Nintendo. But there is a difference: these, by and large, are direct imports from Asia. They are not the legacy of Asian immigrant life. They are cultural memes, transmitted by the image, by the word, by the airwave, by the byte. They don't need human carriers.

It is perhaps unfair to expect Asian Americans to influence American life in the same fashion, to the same degree, as the Jews have. One reason is the ever-quickening pace of assimilation. For all that we hear about the "disuniting of America," the truth is it has never been easier to assimilate than it is today. Ever since the 1960s, new arrivals—at least those with some education—have faced gradually fewer barriers to social entry. They do not have to ghettoize. They are not forced, by the ostracism of others, to sustain and draw sustenance from their heritage. They are freer to adopt other styles, to invent their own.

But the other reason why it is unfair to expect Asian Americans to contribute as a people is simply that Asian Americans are not "a people." They are a label. Great deeds and works can be collected under that label, but the label itself is not much of a muse. As an agent of cultural and social change, the Jew is sui generis; the New Jew, mere proof of that.

———

Whenever I come across an article about the Hmong in Wisconsin or the Hasidim in Brooklyn persisting in their defiance of modernity, insisting on their hermetic ways, I wonder whether I am reading an obituary. In every camp there will be cultural conservationists: those who order their lives around the protection of the past. The most radical are usually the most successful. But their success is arduous, demanding. Even they may not be able to hold out. Even they may eventually be diluted.

"Diluted," of course, is the half-empty view of the glass. "Enriched" is the half-full view. When I think of the many Jewish weddings I've been to, only one was between two Jews. For the others, what else is there but the half-full view?

Ask my Jewish grandmother (all right, grandmother-in-law). Helen Gold Haymon was born in Anchorage, the daughter of Lithuanian Jews who had migrated to America. When her mother died in the great influenza epidemic of 1918, her father gave her up to a Jewish orphanage in New Orleans. She grew up in Louisiana, married a non-Jewish man from Baton Rouge, raised five children, the oldest of whom became the father of the girl I would meet at Yale and marry seven years later. This story is probably beyond what Carroll's great-grandfather, or mine, could have comprehended. But it is not exceptional: that's the point.

During the holiday season, Helen makes an effort to remind her children of the Jewishness in their past. In their blood. It is a fragile remnant now—sometimes a Seder, a few words of Hebrew here and there. It is a remnant that Carroll and I could easily discard. I have a feeling, though, that we will save it. We will weave it into a patchwork of our own, give our children the knowledge, the choice, of continuity. What will people call those children? New Jews, perhaps. New Americans, for certain.

Blood
Vows

1.

In the end we did not incorporate Chinese ritual into our wedding. We had thought about a reading in Mandarin or perhaps some ancient custom that Nai Nai, my father's mother, could tell us about. Something symbolic: A bow to the elders? Incense? Incantations? Nai Nai, who was coming all the way from Taiwan, knew of no such customs still in practice. We asked my mother. Would she like to write something herself, read it from the pulpit? She pondered it awhile. "I don't think so," she answered. "It's too contrived." She wasn't being sardonic. Just stating a fact.

The wedding, in a chapel of dark wood and silver organ pipes, was a symphony of English words: verse, affirmation, Scripture, soprano. Fourth Uncle, my father's brother, whis-

---

pered into Nai Nai's ear as the ceremony unfolded. She nodded slowly.

Carroll and I wrote our own vows. There were seven of them, solemn and plain. The fifth vow bound us "to sustain the cultural traditions we inherit." We spoke it well. But this, of all the covenants we made that day, was the only one that felt like a challenge: an urgent reminder, a plea.

2.

On a chill autumn morning, I sit in a tattered armchair in my living room. For the millionth time, I see a book on the crowded shelf facing me. For the first time in many years, I pull it out of its niche, crack it open. It is a college coursebook, *Written Standard Chinese, Volume Three: An Intermediate Reading Text*, by Parker Po-fei Huang and Hugh Stimson. The book is unmarked, unused. I turn, by chance, to a poem: "Thoughts on a Quiet Night," by Li Bai (701–762).

The words are laid out both in Chinese and in the pinyin romanization:

床 前 明 月 光　chúang qían míng yùe guāng

疑 是 地 上 霜　yí shì dì shàng shuāng

舉 頭 望 明 月　jǔ tóu wàng míng yùe

低 頭 思 故 鄉　dī tóu sī gù xiāng

Beneath the text is a linguist's translation:

bed > in-front-of: bright > moon > light
suspect it-is ground > top > frost
raise head + gaze-at bright > moon
lower head + think-about old > home-town

With the further explanation:

"A > B" means "A modifies B"
"A: B" means "A is the topic, B is the comment"
"A B" means "A is the verb, B is its object"
"A + B" means "A and/or B"

This technical deconstruction ignores the cadence, the artistry, of the original. But somehow, I think, it may do greater justice to the Chineseness of the poem than a more polished, literary rendering. For it conveys the minimalism of the language, the density of what is unspoken.

I read the first line aloud: *chuang qian ming yue guang.* My voice startles me; a bird on the sill takes flight. I clear my throat, knowing instinctively how to adjust: how to make the reading more subtle, more full of the proper feeling. I practice the tones of the next line: *yi shi di shang shuang.* I have a sense, as I breathe, that I've read this poem before, the rising and falling so familiar. Something catches. Without the text now, I continue: *ju tou wang ming yue, di tou si gu xiang.*

I lower my head and think of home.

When I look up, I realize: I know these words. Long ago, as a child, I must have spoken them.

3.

When I was a toddler, just over a year old, my mother had to return to Taiwan. Her father had fallen ill. When she returned a month later with a shorter hairstyle, I no longer knew her. I treated her as if she were a stranger. Mom didn't get upset. She went about her business, talking to Dad, unpacking her bags. A few hours later it dawned on me who this lady was. I waddled over her way, my brow furrowed intently. With a bleat of recognition and an open-mouthed smile, I threw a ball of crumpled paper at her. She scooped me up and held me close.

A few months before my wedding, Mom and Carroll and I went to Baton Rouge for a series of parties. The wedding was going to be on the Yale campus in New Haven, and so this, unofficially, was the Southern round of the festivities. It was mid-April. Everything was abloom, impossibly lush: azaleas, ferns, gardenia. I had been here twice before. It was Mom's first time.

Of course, Mom was already well acquainted with Ava and Cordell, Carroll's parents. They'd met several times, got on really well. And when she arrived in Baton Rouge, everyone she met—neighbors, friends, family—was as friendly as could be. They reached out. Mom, inquisitive and eminently likable, reached right back. Everyone was in good spirits. So it was rather peculiar that within hours of her arrival I began to worry intensely about how happy a time she was having, how well she was fitting in.

Something came over me, a tide of irrationality that I hadn't expected and couldn't fathom. More than once, even when we were just hanging around the house, I came close to tears. I suddenly felt so lonely, so lost. So guilty. As if my mother and I were on a raft and I was plunging into the sea. Everyone was calling her Julia. *Juu-lia.* It sounded funny—not the Louisiana elongation, but the appellation itself: her public name. I realized then how accustomed I'd grown to calling Ava and Cordell "Ava" and "Cordell," their private names. Always, out of the corner of my eye, I checked to see if Mom was feeling left out, ignored. She wasn't. But neither was she entirely her relaxed, at-home self. She was in the role of the guest. I tried to draw her out, to talk to her in her room that night. *Ey Mah!* I tried, in effect, to toss a paper ball at her. She wouldn't play. *Go on,* she said quietly in Chinese, *let's not be rude to our hosts.* When I saw how neatly she had packed her suitcase, my heart ached.

The next night was the first of the parties, a big jambalaya fest thrown by several family friends. There were probably fifty or sixty people there, people who'd known Carroll since she was a child. They clearly were fond of her, and their affection spilled over to Mom and me. The yard was set up with picnic tables, streamers and balloons, coolers full of drink. The evening air was soothing. Even outdoors, the buzz of conversation was loud. Someone put on a CD of Cajun music, accordions and fiddles and achy Gallic choruses. I broke away from a circle of people to look for my mother. A whoop came up from the patio, there was clapping, and then I saw her: she was learning how to two-step, her eyes sparkling and her mouth wide open in delight as her teacher twirled her round. Soon, others were dancing too. I walked over and stood next to Cordell, who was finishing up his plate so he could join the fun. For the first time in days, it seemed, I exhaled. "Boy," said Cordell with a smile, "she sure is light on her feet."

4.

I think about a friend whose Chinese parents will not attend her wedding because her fiancé is black; I talk to another friend whose relationship collapsed because her Chinese parents would not have allowed her to become engaged to her white boyfriend; I recall the dour faces of a different set of Chinese parents who did, grudgingly, permit the marriage; I see all these parents, and I wonder: how did I have it so easy?

My father, actually, would have preferred that I marry a Chinese girl. He said so to my mother once. When Mom told me this recently, I was a bit surprised. I guess I was unaware of how much pride of race he had quietly harbored. What else did I not know? My father had already been gone nearly five years when I was wed. And so it is difficult to imagine just how he and I would have talked about this.

He would not have blocked me, I feel very sure. He probably wouldn't even have expressed his disappointment (though that is not to say I wouldn't have sensed it). I do think he would have liked Carroll a great deal; realized, as Mom did early on, how fundamentally good she is. I suspect also that he would have hit it off with Cordell, both of them being the type to see much more than they let on. But this I cannot truly know of my father. This, now, is beyond my capacity to imagine.

If my father had lived, all things would be different. I know not how nor what person I would be today. I know only that he did not live, that my grief changed me, and that when Carroll and I came together, my mother, to my great relief, was happy for me. Mom had never had much use for the imperatives of racial purity. She took a more romantic view, a view shaped in youth by her reading of Turgenev and Hardy. As long as Carroll and I truly loved each other, that was what mattered most. Such is Mom's nature: to be open; to mix East and West with curiosity and cultivation; to search out that which fastens and connects.

But my mother knows that her liberality—my liberty— must have a cost. She worries that someday, when I have children who may not speak her native tongue, when I have built a life somewhere else, when I have "merged," as she says, "into American society," she and I will drift apart. Of course, I can't imagine that happening. I won't let it. We rarely go two days without talking. I know, though, that when she calls and gets our answering machine, she doesn't leave a message. She doesn't like to intrude.

5.

Let me try to explain why I married a white woman.

It wasn't as if I had a plan. I wasn't trying to prove a point or to defy convention. It was simply a matter of who was there and what was possible. Why did Carroll marry a Chinese man? Why do people of different races marry at all? For the same reason today that they go to school together, live together, travel together, work together: because they can.

Most of the women I have encountered in my life have been white. Most, but not all, of those I have found attractive have also been white. And most who found me attractive were white as well. What does this all mean? What *should* it mean? How much of this pattern is chance? How much, the product of unseen forces?

I have never consciously placed Asian women or any class of women out of bounds, beyond attraction. But then, attraction isn't really the province of the conscious, rational mind.

The theory is that I was influenced by the messages of the

dominant culture: the magazine covers, the pinup posters, the smiling faces on television. The theory is that I was brainwashed into believing that white beauty is the only true beauty and was therefore dedicated to seeking out the same. The theory is that I've had to fight all my life against the stereotype of the emasculated Asian male and thus needed to have a white wife to set things right.

I won't deny that the culture shapes me in unseen ways. Did a habit of downplaying racial difference influence my idea of female attractiveness? I don't dismiss the possibility. But I am reluctant, in the end, to call myself a simple slave to the subliminal, the mere sum of my fears.

I *chose.* I chose to enter into a relationship with Carroll. Not with "a white woman," not with some nameless paragon of "white beauty," but with Carroll Haymon, who has always had an uncanny knack for finishing my sentences; who knows when to humor me and when not to; who, as a southerner schooled in the North, is no stranger to acculturation; whose neck bends just so when she reads; who sings a soulful alto and scorns the designated-hitter rule; who has a way of putting complete strangers completely at ease. Nobody—and nobody's subconscious—tricked me into falling in love with her.

Today, when racial intermarriage is rising but still not the rule, it is tempting to read every mixed coupling as a text: on sexual politics, on the relative worth of skin hues, on the hidden insecurities of one spouse or another. To some people, the idea that love is more than skin deep sounds suspiciously like a pretext. To some people, there must always be an ulterior motive.

Sometimes, yes, love of another is but a mutation of self-loathing. Sometimes wedlock is the highest form of denial. But sometimes, to paraphrase Freud, a marriage is just a marriage.

6.

"What made me Mexican?" asks the writer Ilan Stavans in *The Hispanic Condition*. "It's hard to know: language and the air I breathed, perhaps."

My wife and my mother both contend that I have a strong streak of Chinese in me, in my way of being. Carroll cites the following as evidence: I keep things close; I don't like to have house guests; I worry about appearances; I am loyal to family; I am a responsible elder child; I work hard; I resist change in small things; I think Chinese food is superior. Mom locates my Chineseness elsewhere: in my respect for Chinese culture, in my sense of personal balance, in my understanding of obligation and duty.

I wonder. Perhaps what Carroll sees in me is mainly my mother, and what my mother sees in me is mainly my father. I'll happily agree that I am very much like my parents. But this only pushes the inquiry back one generation: What part of them is Chinese? What part of them is them?

On one level, Chineseness is the idiom of my every memory of family life. It is the sound of my father's bamboo slippers as he climbed up the stairs at night. It is the cadence of conversations with grandparents whom I could comprehend only intermittently. It is the colorful stacks of Chinese newspapers that were all but indecipherable to me. It is the smell of ginger and scallions frying in a blackened wok. It is the little red envelopes that promised crisp ten-dollar bills every Christmas.

Beyond this, though, I struggle to articulate just what Chineseness means. The air I breathed? I try to imagine what memories of home life my children will have. What shall I preserve for them? Moon cakes for the autumn-harvest festival, sweet, sticky *niangao* at the Chinese New Year, *hongbao*— those little red envelopes—for every special occasion. Yes, these I shall preserve.

But are customs ever enough? Customs alone are mere symbols, distillations, as distinct from cultural truth as water is from vapor. We will need language also. We will need it centrally. For it is in the sound of the language, the aspirates, the curling of the tongue, the mode of thought that the grammar demands, that this phantom I call Chineseness will truly take form—if it ever will.

Here is where the balance teeters. When I am chatting with my mother, 80 percent of her words are Chinese and only 10 percent of mine. But the English I use isn't standard English. It's Chinese verbs and English conjugations, or vice versa. Or it's an American phrase with a playful twist by Mom: "Just come," for example, is the correct response to "How come?" And "Hi, dots!"—the way Mom once interpreted "Hey, dudes!"—is now our standard greeting. We speak like children who haven't yet been confined by the rules of proper syntax. We speak what comes most easily. As a result, I know only enough Chinese to know that I've been a careless custodian. What mongrelized, vestigial argot will I bequeath to the next generation?

Every year I promise myself and my mother that I will *buxi*—repair—my Chinese skills. Every year I promise, believing blithely that I will find those elusive few months to take a refresher course, that once I'm back up to speed everything will be OK: the fray will be mended, the lack made full, and the word made knowable to my children. But how, exactly? How, when Carroll and I will speak nothing but English in the kitchen every day, when what my mother and I speak is not even really Chinese anymore?

One night, after dinner, Carroll says that when the time comes, she'd like our children to attend Chinese school. I pause, and think to myself: That's *my* line.

7.

We have a friend with the wonderfully German name Berndt Schmidt. He grew up in the Midwest, went to college in Minnesota. Six foot plus, brownish hair. He is a physician now. Dr. Schmidt. When he was a boy, Berndt spent a few months in China. He picked up some Mandarin, learned the rhythms of the village, played games, did chores. He lived with a Chinese family. He lived, actually, with his mother's sister and his first cousins.

Not long ago Berndt and his wife, Julie, came over to have dinner and to look at photographs. First Carroll and I showed them the several rolls we'd taken on our honeymoon in China: Tiananmen Square, the Great Wall, our cruise ship on the Yangzi River, the Three Gorges, the famous Shanghai shopping district. Then Berndt showed us the boxful of pictures from his summer many years ago: old men playing Chinese chess, his aunty at the market, children running around a courtyard. One of those children is him.

Berndt can no longer speak the language. He hasn't been back to China. If you look at him, you might not impute much significance to the slightly almond shape of his eyes, the wiriness of his hair. Generally, people don't assume he is Chinese. He can pretty well pass for white. But it is safe to say that he is as interested in his Chinese half as I am in my Chinese whole. Which makes me feel ... what? That I have taken far too much for granted.

I'd like to know: Who is Chinese American? Who is Asian American? Once upon a time that was a straightforward inquiry. But the 1990 census, which is already ancient history, reveals why the question grows ever more nettlesome: Among

Asian Americans between age twenty-five and thirty-four, exactly 50 percent of the men were married to non-Asians, and 55 percent of the women. Among Asian Americans *under* twenty-five, it was 54 percent of the men, 66 percent of the women.

What will "Asian American" mean when a majority of the next generation is of mixed parentage? Will membership in the race depend more on heredity or on heritage? Chromosomes or culture? Will it be a matter of voluntary affiliation, a question of choice? Or will the "one-drop rule" that makes American blacks black make anyone with an Asian ancestor Asian? Who will pass for white—and who will want to?

At a high school I visit, a Chinese/Irish boy complains that he feels left out of the Asian American activities. On another campus, a black/Japanese girl is the head of the Asian student organization. There are no rules of thumb. There is no way to predict.

It is possible that the Asian American identity, fragile invention that it is, will simply dissipate through intermarriage, as so many Jews fear is happening to their community. On the other hand, it's possible that the Asian identity will intensify in the next generation. Sometimes the most fervent believers in the power of colored blood are those of mixed ancestry. Meanwhile, *intra*-Asian marriages—among Indian and Filipino and Korean and other Asian Americans—are also dramatically on the rise. The old borders are shifting. Where they will settle— or whether—there is simply no way to predict.

Take two Americans: one, proficient in Korean, a devotee of John Woo films, practitioner of Ayurvedic healing, follower of Taoism; the other, blissfully ignorant of all of the above. Which one is more Asian? Would it matter which one was "actually"—that is, genetically—more Asian? Culture is breaking loose from the moorings of race. Phenotype is becoming an unreliable indicator of privileged knowledge. There is no way to predict.

An article in *Amerasia Journal*, published by UCLA's Asian American Studies Center, describes the "phenomenology" of *hapa* identity at a Los Angeles high school. The author, Jeff Yoshimi, interviews teens with the following names: Sean McKean, Nye Liu, Renard Dubois, Lih Russell, Bruce Moore, Midori Nakano, Cindy and Susan Fowler, Courtney Hannah, Tracey Stokes. They all seem unaware of how aware they are of race. Do you want to guess which of them are multiracial? Dare you order them by Asianness of look? Asianness of self-concept? "What *are* you?" these students are asked. There is no way to predict.

I am Tiger Woods. Everyone knows that Tiger is multiracial. Not everyone knows he is more Asian than anything else. His father is half African American, one quarter Native American, and one quarter Chinese; his mother is half Thai, one quarter Chinese, and one quarter white. When Tiger-mania first began to swell, I fully expected Woods to be marketed as The Great Black Hope. For a while he was. But then, remarkably, the media machinery switched gears. They figured it out:

his is the face of our intermingled future. *I am Tiger Woods,* say now the fays of Nike and Benneton and Calvin Klein. Who knows just how color will be commodified next century? There is no way to predict.

I am of a transitional generation, one that is still struck, bemused, moved, by the novelty of a half-Chinese man named Schmidt who has known China better than I may ever know it. I am of a generation that can say the words but not fully grasp their meaning: Race is falling apart. Collapsing into complexity. As a magnificent Stanley Crouch essay puts it, "Race Is Over."

Realize, though, that race is over, obsolete, only in a very specific sense: As a predictor. As a proxy. Face value—the assignment of moral and cultural meaning to slanted eyes or thick lips or a flat nose—is losing value every day. But what remains, in spite of this fact, is a deeply ingrained instinct for classification. (What *are* you?) What remains is this truth: a world where the colors run is still not a world where the colors run equally.

8.

The "Negro problem," wrote Norman Podhoretz in 1963, would not be solved unless color itself disappeared: "and that means not integration, it means assimilation, it means—let the brutal word come out—miscegenation." Coming after a lengthy confession of his tortured feelings toward blacks—and coming at a time when nineteen states still had antimiscegenation statutes on the books—Podhoretz's call for a "wholesale merging of the two races" seemed not just bold but desperate. Politics had failed us, he was conceding; now we could find hope only in the unlikely prospect of intermarriage.

Podhoretz's famous essay was regarded as peculiar at the time, but today it seems like prophecy. We are intermarrying in unprecedented numbers. Between 1970 and 1992 the number of mixed-race marriages quadrupled. We are mixing our genes with such abandon that the Census Bureau considered adding a new "multiracial" category to the forms in the year 2000. It settled instead on a potentially more radical solution: allowing people to check as many boxes as they wish.

These changes have provoked strong reactions from civil rights activists who fear that many minorities will defect from their old categories, thus diluting colored political clout. But the debate, properly framed, isn't about "light flight." It's about our very conception of race. For the new rules are an admission that the five points of what David Hollinger calls the "ethnoracial pentagon" (black, white, Asian, Hispanic, Native American) aren't fixed or divinely ordained, but fickle and all too man-made.

Race, you see, is a fiction. As a matter of biology it has no meaningful basis. Genetic variations within any race far exceed the variations between the races, and genetic similarities among the races swamp both. The power of race, however, derives not from its pseudoscientific markings but from its social trappings. It is as an *ideology* that race matters, indeed matters so much that the biologists' protestations fall away like Copernican claims in the age of Ptolemy.

The hope is that the emergence of a mixed-race community will help obliterate our antiquated notions of racial difference. I'm all for that. I certainly won't want to infect my Chinese-Scottish-Irish-Jewish children with bloodline fever. I won't force them to choose among ill-fitting racial uniforms. That said, though, there is reason to wonder whether miscegenation alone can ever, as one commentator put it, "blow the lid off of race."

Foremost is this reality: racialism is awfully adaptive. No matter how quickly demographics change, we seem to find a way to sustain our jerry-built pigmentocracy. Take the term "Hispanic." Ever since it was added to the census in 1977, we've been told that "Hispanic" is merely a linguistic category, that Hispanics "can be of any race." Today, amid a boom in the Hispanic population, we hear that caveat the same way smokers read the surgeon general's warning. Heterogeneous Hispanics—who ought to have exposed the flimsiness of racial categories—became in the popular mind just another homogeneous race.

Could this happen to people of mixed descent? Their very

existence as a group is premised on the idea of *transcending* race. Moreover, they have less reason to cohere than Hispanics ever had: they include every conceivable combination of genes and are not bound together by another language. Still, in a nation accustomed to thinking of "official races," people of mixed descent could come to be regarded as a bloc of their own.

One possibility is that multiracials, over time, will find themselves deemed a middleman race. Their presence, like that of the "coloreds" in old South Africa, wouldn't undermine racialism; it would reinforce it, by fleshing out a rough white-black caste system. Again, however, the sheer diversity of the multiracial population would probably prevent this from happening.

Yet this same diversity makes it possible that multiracials will replicate within their ranks the "white-makes-right" mentality that prevails all around them. Thus we might see a hierarchy take hold in which a mixed child with "white" blood would be the social better of a mixed child without such blood. In this scenario, multiracials wouldn't be a distinct group; they'd be distributed across a continuum of color.

Perhaps such a continuum is preferable to a simple black-white dichotomy. Brazilians, for instance, with their many gradations of *tipo*, or "type," behold with disdain our crude bifurcation of race. But no amount of baloney-slicing changes the fact that, in Brazil, whitening remains the ideal. It is still better for a woman to be a *branca* (light skin, hair without tight curls, thin lips, narrow nose) than a *morena* (tan skin, wavy hair, thicker lips, broader nose); and better to be a *morena* than a *mulata* (darker skin, tightly curled hair). Subverting racial labels is not the same as subverting racism.

Still another possibility is that whites will do to the multiracials what the Democrats or Republicans have traditionally done to third-party movements: absorb their most "desirable" elements and leave the rest on the fringe. It's quite possible, as the sociologist Mary Waters suggests, that the ranks of the white will simply expand to include the "lighter" or more "culturally white" of the multiracials.

All these scenarios, far-fetched as they may sound, should remind us that our problem isn't just "race" in the abstract; it's the idea of the "white race" in particular. So long as we speak of whiteness as the social norm and "passing" as the option of choice, no amount of census reshuffling will truly matter.

We return, then, to the question of politics. Perhaps we should abolish racial classification altogether. Perhaps we need more class-based variants of affirmative action. Perhaps we need a form of national service to counter the effects of resegregation. Whatever it takes, though, we need to do more than marry one another if we are ever to rid our society of color-consciousness. "The way of politics," Podhoretz lamented, "is slow and bitter." Indeed. But it is the only lasting way. Our ideology of "blood," like blood itself, is too fluid, too changeable, and too easily diverted to be remade by lovers alone.

9.

I've been thinking a lot about Chinese babies lately. They're cute, perhaps the cutest kind of baby (of course, *I'd* think that). They're also a rather hot item now on the adoption markets. The one-child policy in China, the ingrained preference there for boys, the rise in childless couples here with the means and wherewithal to adopt—all have contributed to a dramatic rise in the number of Chinese-born adoptees in the United States. At last count, according to A. *Magazine,* there were about twelve thousand, up from a mere handful in 1990.

Whenever I read an article about Asian adoptees, whenever I see a photo of an Asian child with her white parents or siblings, smiling, at home, I feel a tinge of sadness. Perhaps that's because the act of adoption is itself tinged with sadness. Or perhaps it's because on some unseen plane I can envision what an adopted Asian child must go through to live an American life.

What is it like to be cut off from a past, to be born as if there is no past? What obligation do your parents bear to expose you to the ways of the old country? To bequeath memory unto you, where none existed before? To unfold life's lessons in the same patterns, the same strokes and catechisms, that another set of parents in another time and place might have used?

And you—what obligation do you incur? To live not only the life you have—the school bus, the birthday party, the instant memory of the camcorder—but also the life you never had? To link yourself to a chain of greater meaning? What duty have you to reconnect the cord—and if not a duty, then what desire?

These are the questions I would ask an Asian child raised by a Caucasian family. They are the very questions I sometimes ask myself.

A self-indulgent pose, I know: I *have* a history, I *have* blood parents, I *have* a kind of access to the past that an adoptee does not. How can I make our situations equivalent? I can't. I don't. Though I suffer slightly from glaucoma of the memory, I do not labor in the darkness that shrouds the adoptee. If I chose to, I could reverse the creeping blindness.

But what if I chose not to? Think of the next generation. Imagine if I chose to raise children in total ignorance of their Chinese kinfolk. I wouldn't, but imagine if I chose to offer them only plates of silence when they began to hunger for heritage. Imagine if I chose never to burden them with the weight of history, the very history that had made them possible. Would they still find a way, in spite of my choice? Would they throw off this yoke of the present, the now, the tomorrow, and meander back to a distant Chineseness: to their roots?

Children are not cut from whole cloth: they bear the threads of other fabrics. They do not come into the world wholly autonomous: they are born into many systems of commitment. Yet I cannot imagine forcing children of my own to adopt any single way of being. I cannot imagine requiring them to be very Chinese or not at all Chinese. I will give *them* the choice. But before that, I will give them the ability to know why they choose. They will learn how their family came to be, from what corners of the world their ancestors sprang, what tongues and rituals once flourished under their names. They will be exposed to their inheritance—even, I hope, that part of the inheritance I have let fall into disuse. And they will decide.

These may sound like liberal views, but in a sense they are as conservative as can be: I only want to raise my offspring as I myself was raised. It just happens that I was raised with great latitude—to preserve, discard, combine, and create. My parents may not have realized the danger of such a course. The danger was that I would never look back. But I do. I do, constantly. I learned a lesson they may not even have meant to teach: that freedom, well nurtured, can grow to fidelity. And so I, too, will pass something on: language, food, custom, and, most important, trust.

There is an old home movie, a scratchy 8-mm Kodak film, that plays in the dark hollow of my head some nights. It belongs to Ava and Cordell, and it is the sort of evidence one might marshal to prove the existence of Destiny. In the movie, Carroll is maybe six years old. Her hair is a small swirl of orange, her skin plush and pale. Her accent is more pronounced than I've ever known it to be. And she is learning to speak Chinese. I don't know what inspired Ava to have her daughter schooled so. Anyway, what little of the language Carroll knew then, she soon forgot. But somehow, we all believe, certain pathways were laid down. Word by word, Carroll learned something. Frame by frame, I see it unfold: The tutor, a Chinese graduate student at LSU, sits on the floor across from Carroll. She asks Carroll a question—about milk, I think. And in a Mandarin bent by a child's Louisiana drawl, Carroll answers.

10.

In the summer after college, my father and mother taught me how to stir-fry. They taught me some of my favorite dishes, simple ABC favorites like beef and broccoli or corn and pork (never more than two constituent elements)—dishes I'd be able to make for myself when I moved to Washington.

I learned first by watching. I had seen them make dinner thousands of times, but never had I really watched. Then I learned by writing everything down. Meticulously, as if producing a scientific outline:

A.   1. wash meat → pat dry (½ lb beef).
       2. cut into strips *along* grain → cut out white fat
       3. cut into slices *perpendicular* to grain (fingertips curled down)

And so forth. I wanted to get it exactly right. I pressed them to specify, down to the half-teaspoon, how much soy sauce, how much corn starch, how many seconds on high heat. They didn't really know. *We just made it up—we don't keep track.* So they offered some rough numbers. I recorded them dutifully. Finally, my notes complete (F.1. Eat!), I learned by doing. Mom stood beside me, apron on, telling me when to add the vegetables, when to use water, how to wield the spatula.

In that first year of life in the "real world," which was the last year before my father died, I got pretty good at making those dishes. I was given a wok of my own and a rice cooker. I accumulated a stash of sauces and spices. I cooked for my roommates. Once, when my mother visited, I cooked for her. She liked it. At first I read those recipes the way a rabbinical student reads the Talmud. I kept them right next to me on the counter, followed them to the letter. But as time passed, the patterns slipped. The more I cooked, the less I relied on the original formulas. Some steps I began to do by memory. Others I began to revise, adapt, invent. Always, I added more sugar than I should have.

These days it is Carroll who handles most of the cooking, even the Chinese-style cooking, which she will do out of the *Moosewood Cookbook* or *Greens, Glorious Greens!* But every now and then, when we have a craving for chicken and tomato, say, or beef and broccoli, I will go to the file cabinet in my study and pull out those oil-stained, curled-at-the-corner pieces of paper. I don't need them the way I once did. I turn to them mainly to reorient myself, so that before I fill my kitchen again with the scents of home I might remember what it is I have forgotten. That much, at least, I have promised to do.

11.

Epiphany stops time.

I have opened an illuminated manuscript. *The Book of Mechtilde,* inspired by the Book of Job, is a painstaking work of remembrance by a young Caribbean-born artist named Anna Ruth Henriques. She created it to honor her mother, Sheila Mechtilde Chong Henriques. She composed it in her own hand, though clearly, as Simon Schama writes in a review, her hand is more than her own: it belongs also to a Chinese grandmother, to the Jamaican Sephardic Jews of her father's family, to the nuns at a Franciscan school, to the clear air and light of an Afro-Atlantic isle. On the even-numbered pages, a simple poetic rendering of her mother's life and death. On the odd-numbered pages, the most arresting illustrations: golden threads of Scripture spun tightly around a spool of richly hued iconic imagery. To read the verse, one must turn the book round and round, the wheel of revelation at once centripetal and centrifugal. *What knowest thou, that we know not? What understandeth thou, which is not in us?*

I wonder, as I stare slack-jawed at this text in the local bookstore: Who among us is truly pure?

I do not celebrate the hybrid out of blind faith. The commingling of bloodlines is often cheerfully said to produce the "best of many worlds." But there is no reason, really, why it cannot produce the very worst of those worlds. What matters is how, and why, and with what care, the many parts are made whole.

Is the end product of American life, of assimilation, a mere molten lump? This is what the preservationists fear: the Chinese parents who will not countenance their child's love of another, the Jewish leaders who decry the secularization of their heritage, the multicultural identity sovereigns who insist on *keeping it real*. But the choice, in fact, is not between real and fake. It is not between the pure and the despoiled. It is about what degree of in-between, which of the innumerable possible combinations, what sort of synthesis we will bring into being.

Think about whose words are on your mind, whose palate you taste with, whose song you hum, whose slang you sling, whose rites you observe. Are they black? Are they Hispanic? Are they Jewish? Are they Asian? Are they Creole, mestizo? The end product of American life is not some bland blank slate; it is a palimpsest, page upon storied page of illuminated manuscript. The end product of American life is neither monoculturalism nor multiculturalism; it is *omniculturalism*.

Early in the century a Mexican philosopher named José Vasconcelos wrote an essay called *La Raza Cosmica* (The Cosmic Race). Vasconcelos predicted that the wholesale merging of the many races would soon lead to a new stage of human consciousness and usher in an era of peace, beauty, and love. Perhaps he was a bit overoptimistic. But we don't have to share every tenet of his expansive faith to recognize that something cosmic *is* happening in this country. Ours is a land of borderlands, the frontier of frontiers: we mix, that others in the world may imagine.

What happens here, of course, is not *inherently* blessed. It is only the future.

12.

On the eve of my wedding my mother presents to Carroll and me a thin album. For the first time, she has gathered together all the old photographs of her family and my father's family: Stern great-grandparents frozen in sepia. A coquettish girl in Western dress (Po-Po), her black-and-white image touched with color. A proud aging man in uniform and his fresh-faced son, who is my father. A pretty schoolgirl in a scout's uniform: my mother. She has made a document of my history. She has left the last several pages blank.

On the day of the wedding, Ava, who is a poet, bestows another gift upon us. In that chapel of dark wood and silver organ pipes, before all the family and friends who have gathered close, Ava reads the epithalamion, the matrimonial ode, she has composed for us. It is a lyric poem, given lyrically. It tells of the parents' pride: *Your daring wakens our courage.* It whispers the parents' grief: *we have known you so well until now.* It conjures up myth and enchantment and the fairy tale version of connubial bliss. It ends, as all things begin, with a covenant:

We release you. Our own fairy tale compels us.
We will not ask you to realize our ambitions,
To exact our revenges, to redeem our mistakes.
Our hands are open. We give you our blessing.
Go. Make up your own story.

This book is the product of many conversations. The earliest were with Rafe Sagalyn, my literary agent, and Jon Karp, my editor at Random House. Rafe pushed me to form my ideas; his savvy counsel was indispensable. Jon helped conceive of this project, and he guided me through it with wisdom, skill, and always just the right kind of encouragement. I deeply appreciate the faith they've both shown in me.

Among those who gave generously of their time, and whose thoughts influenced mine (sometimes in dissent), are Jon Alter, K. Anthony Appiah, Jenny Lyn Bader, Tina Bennett, Jonathan Cohn, Debra Dickerson, Trinh Duong, Jim Fallows, Francis Fukuyama, Bill Galston, Henry Louis Gates, Jr., Emil Guillermo, J. D. Hokoyama, Noel Ignatiev, Randall Kennedy, Mike Kinsley, Harold Koh, Peter Kwong, Chuck Lane, Chang-rae Lee, Mike Lind, Kollin Min, Clarence Page, Jeremy Rosner, Jack Shafer, Jeff Shesol, Judith Shulevitz, Rick Stengel, David Tang, Shawn Wong, Frank Wu, Alice Young, Grace Yuan, Judy Yu, and Fareed Zakaria.

Some material in this book grew out of pieces that appeared in *Slate*, *The Washington Post Magazine*, *USA Weekend*, and *MSNBC Interactive*. I wish to thank the editors at these publications who sharpened my ideas and prose.

At Random House, Sally Marvin, Andy Carpenter, Sono Rosenberg, Sean Abbott and Monica Gomez worked hard to make this book happen.

I am also indebted to several people who read and critiqued the manuscript. Jeff Yang is an exacting reader and candid friend. Angelo Ragaza's subtlety I came to know firsthand. David Greenberg has the eye and ear of a master editor. Dana Milbank provided a multitude of insightful comments. Glenn Loury identified exactly how the book could be improved. Annie Boyer fortified both the manuscript and me at a critical time. Ava and Cordell Haymon offered sage advice and a more profound knowledge of family.

My wife, my soul mate, Carroll Haymon, read and revised every page of every draft. She knew what I was trying to say, knew when I wasn't saying it. She tolerated my midnight bursts of activity and my writerly mood swings. But more than all that, and long before this book had even been imagined, Carroll did something else: she opened my heart, and enabled me to speak of it.

When I think of all the conversations that shaped these pages, I think in the end of those with my mother, Julia Liu. Always, Mom told me honestly how my words made her feel. Always, she gave me her unconditional love. Anyone who knows Mom well knows of her talent for questions, her disregard for boundary, her will to fathom herself. Anyone who knows me well knows how thankful I am to be my mother's son.

ERIC LIU, twenty-nine, has been a speechwriter for President Bill Clinton and a commentator for MSNBC. A regular contributor to *Slate*, he has also written for *The Washington Post Magazine*, and *USA Weekend*. After founding *The Next Progressive*, an acclaimed journal of opinion, he edited the anthology *Next: Young American Writers on the New Generation*. He is a graduate of Yale College, and is now enrolled at Harvard Law School.

ABOUT THE TYPE

This book was set in Electra, a typeface designed for Linotype by W. A. Dwiggins, the renowned type designer (1880–1956). Electra is a fluid typeface, avoiding the contrasts of thick and thin strokes that are prevalent in most modern typefaces.